Leadership Unlocked: 10 Keys to Influence and Impact

James Rodriguez

Copyright ©2025 JAMES RODRIGUEZ

All rights reserved.

No portion of this book may be reproduced in any form without written permission from the publisher or author, except as permitted by U.S. copyright law.

Dedication

To God, who gave me purpose.

To my daughters, Brianna Herrera and Serenidad Smith, who gave me motivation and remind me daily of what true love and legacy look like.

To my mom, Rebecca Candal, who showed me through her example that no matter what your situation is, you can overcome it and grow.

To my brother and sister, Herminio and Zenaida Rodriguez—I also dedicate this book to you. You went through all the early struggles with me as children and teenagers, and you've both become incredible human beings and parents. I love you both!

To my granddaughters, Elaina and Vera Herrera, Ava Carter, and Harley Smith—may God bless you and guide you all in your own journeys of leadership.

And to every leader who dares to grow—this book is for you.

Acknowledgments

I want to begin by thanking all those who have allowed me to lead or mentored me along the way. In more ways than you may realize, you've each contributed to my journey of growth and leadership. I am truly honored to have had the opportunity to lead and to learn from you. To my daughter, Brianna Herrera—your constant support and belief in this book and me have meant the world. You are my greatest motivation, my "why," and the heart behind this book. To my uncle and aunt, Remi and Raquel Acosta—though you are no longer with us, your presence continues to guide me. Remi, you were like a father to me through my teenage years and into adulthood. Your lives were examples of strength, love, and faith. You may be gone, but you still live within my heart and my mind. To John C. Maxwell—thank you for shaping my thinking and leadership in the early 1990s through your books, and later through your audio teachings. In 2012, when I became a certified coach on your Leadership Team, your mentorship became even more personal. You've consistently added value to my life and to countless others. I'm deeply grateful. To Glenn and Sheri Brooks—thank you for encouraging me to take what I had been writing for years off the shelf and finally get it done. Your belief in me gave me the final push I needed to bring this message to life. To everyone who has shaped me—my middle and high school teachers, my college professors, my military leaders, the many managers I've worked with (both good and bad), my business partners, and to all my family and friends—thank you for the lessons, the challenges, the love, and the growth. This book is not mine alone. It's a reflection of all of you.

Table of Contents

1. The Road to Leadership
2. The Key of the Mirror
3. The Key of Self-Belief
4. The Key of Direction
5. The Key of Great Communication
6. The Key of Follow-Up
7. The Key of Recruiting with the End in Mind
8. The Key of Trust
9. The Key of Living from Solutions
10. The Key of Adding Value
11. The Key of 7x Advanced Leadership
12. Final Reflection: The Heart Behind This Book
13. About the Author

Chapter 1

The Road to Leadership

When I reflect on how I arrived at where I am today, I realize the journey has been anything but linear. I was born in Brooklyn and raised in East Harlem, New York, during the gritty backdrop of the 1970s—a time and place where survival often depended on street smarts and community bonds. In 1980, I relocated to Connecticut, but my formative years—the years that truly shaped me—were grounded in the streets of East Harlem.

My mother was just 14 years old when I was born. By 18, she was already raising three children—me, my younger brother, and my sister. Our parents did what they could with what they had. My father, having grown up without the guidance of a father himself and lacking any formal education, relied on the streets to teach him. And in turn, the streets became our classroom too. He passed on what he had learned—resilience, toughness, and how to navigate a world that wasn't built to support us.

East Harlem wasn't just a neighborhood. It was a tribe, a living organism of families that looked out for one another. On 108th Street, between First and Second Avenues, everyone knew each other. We shared more than just space—we shared responsibility. By the time I was 12, I was already navigating an environment where street gangs were on the rise, targeting kids in and around JHS 45, where I attended school on 120th Street.

Faced with growing threats, my friends and I decided we couldn't just be victims—we needed to organize. We strategized, united by the desire to protect ourselves and our community. Out of this came the **Latin Crew-Saders of East Harlem**. I was just 13 years old, the youngest of the four founding members. This was my first real experience with leadership. Not in theory, not in a classroom—but in the raw reality of street-level decision-making, influence, and loyalty.

What started as a small neighborhood crew grew rapidly. We expanded to Brooklyn, the Bronx, Queens, and even Connecticut. I became fascinated by the idea of leadership—why some people naturally commanded respect, while others couldn't inspire even the smallest following. I didn't yet understand the mechanics of influence, but I was learning through fire.

By age 14, I was deeply entrenched in gang life. Our world was marked by territorial clashes, late-night parties in city parks, and the rise of hip-hop that pulsed through the streets. I was there when our crews gathered in Jefferson Park for a city-wide summit of gangs—a moment that, years later, would eerily mirror a scene in *The Warriors*. That meeting felt larger than life. It showed me the potential of unity, even among those seen as outsiders or threats.

But that life came at a cost. We lost a close friend to gun violence, and cracks began to form within our own ranks. At 15, standing at a personal crossroads, I made a life-altering decision: I left it all behind. I moved to Waterbury, Connecticut, to live with my grandmother and two aunts. I left behind the streets, the colors, the identity I had built—and enrolled in my second year of high school with a fresh start.

But leadership didn't leave me. It followed me.

In school, I gravitated toward programs like Junior Achievement and DECA—both centered around business, strategy, and leadership. These opportunities were different from my past, but the core principles were the same: influence, vision, organization. Despite the promise these programs offered, my life remained unstable. My grandmother fulfilled her dream of returning to Puerto Rico. My aunts moved on with their lives. By the end of my junior year in 1982, I found myself alone again—no safety net, no clear direction.

What I did have, though, was my love for water. Swimming had always been my escape. The rhythm of it gave me clarity. Around that time, military recruiters began visiting my high school. Most branches didn't appeal to me—until I heard about the **United States Coast Guard**. They had a unique rule: if you scored at a college level on their entrance exam, you could enlist even without a high school diploma—just parental consent.

At 16, I was determined to change my life. My mother was reluctant, but I convinced her. On July 17, 1982, I turned 17. By August 2, I was standing in Coast Guard boot camp. I was no longer a kid from the block. I was a seaman recruit—and that decision would change my life forever.

Boot camp opened my eyes. It quickly became clear how much I didn't know about the world. By October, I was stationed aboard the **USCGC Midgett (WHEC-726)**, a high-endurance cutter, the Coast Guard's version of a Navy frigate. Some of my fellow recruits went to our sister ship, the USCGC Sherman. I was now part of something bigger, more structured—and more demanding.

One of my earliest culture shocks came when a white shipmate from the South told me, "You're a cool Puerto Rican. Where I'm from, Puerto Ricans and rednecks don't get along." I remember actually looking at his neck, trying to figure out what he meant. I had never encountered that kind of cultural divide growing up in East Harlem. It was the first time I realized how different the world outside my bubble could be.

I served on the Midgett for almost two years. I did well, often excelling in my duties. But inside, I wrestled with a persistent insecurity—I still didn't have a high school diploma. I couldn't shake the feeling that, no matter how well I performed, I was somehow less than. That missing piece haunted me.

But I didn't let it define me. I applied for **A-School**, the Coast Guard's technical training program. At 18, I became the youngest member of my class—and I was appointed **Class Leader**. I graduated second in my class, an accomplishment that confirmed what I had always sensed: leadership was in me. I just needed to embrace it.

From the streets of East Harlem to the decks of a Coast Guard cutter, my journey had already spanned extremes. And yet, I knew—I was only getting started.

Meet the Author: Coach James Rodriguez

James Rodriguez was born in Brooklyn and raised in East Harlem, where the seeds of leadership were planted early in life—often in unlikely and unforgiving environments. From his earliest days navigating the streets of New York to leading high-performing teams across industries and continents, James' journey is a testament to transformation, purpose, and the power of personal growth.

Before he became a recognized leadership coach, speaker, and business strategist, James served six years in the **United States Coast Guard**, a formative period that laid the foundation for his discipline, resilience, and problem-solving mindset. The Coast Guard gave him structure, exposure to diversity, and an education in leadership that transcended any textbook.

After completing his service, James transitioned into the **hospitality and restaurant industry**—starting, humbly, as an assistant manager. But true leaders don't stay small for long. His relentless drive, deep understanding of people, and passion for developing others propelled him up the ranks. Over the next two decades, James would rise through roles including General Manager, District Manager, Director of Operations, and Vice President in multiple sectors, including energy, marketing, and international hospitality. Ultimately, he became **Chief Operating Officer** of a Latin American hospitality group.

Throughout his career, James built a reputation as a **turnaround expert**—a leader who not only drives profits but transforms culture. He doesn't lead from behind a desk. He leads from the front, with authenticity, empathy, and intensity. Whether he's restructuring a struggling team or launching new locations in unfamiliar markets, James has one guiding principle: **"People first. Leadership always."**

The John Maxwell Influence

In the mid-1990s, James encountered a philosophy that would deeply impact his leadership journey: the teachings of **John C. Maxwell**, one of the world's foremost experts on leadership. Maxwell's values-based, servant-leadership principles resonated with James at a soul level. They gave language to what he had already been doing—and vision to what he could become.

James not only applied Maxwell's teachings to his own teams but eventually became a **Certified John Maxwell Coach, Speaker, and Trainer**. Through this work, he began coaching others—executives, managers, and aspiring leaders—guiding them to unlock their potential using both Maxwell's principles and his own hard-earned insights.

In 2018, James had the honor of serving as one of the **leadership coaches for the John Maxwell Team in Costa Rica**, contributing to a nationwide leadership transformation initiative. That experience reinforced a truth he had always believed: **Leadership transcends borders. It doesn't matter where you come from—great leadership changes lives.**

Transforming Leadership in Panama

In recent years, James took his passion and vision to Panama, where he served as **President of Operations for an international hospitality company**. The task? Launch multiple successful restaurants in a country where many had written off the workforce as "unmotivated" or "incapable." But James saw something different.

Where others saw limitations, he saw untapped potential. He worked directly with local staff, breaking through limiting beliefs about what Panamanian employees could achieve. His approach was hands-on, culturally intelligent, and built on trust.

Many local business owners had accepted mediocrity as a cultural trait. James challenged that narrative head-on. He proved that **leadership—not location—determines results**. Under his direction, these restaurants didn't just succeed—they thrived. They won awards. They shattered sales records. They created work environments where people showed up inspired.

His message to business owners across Panama was clear:

"It's not the culture that limits performance—it's the lack of leadership. But to lead effectively, you must **first understand the culture and the people**. Only then can you apply Emotional Intelligence, structure, and strategy to create results."

James' work in Panama solidified his reputation as one of the region's most in-demand consultants and keynote speakers. His leadership style bridges both logic and heart, strategy and soul.

Awards and Recognitions

Throughout his career, James Rodriguez has received numerous accolades for his **transformational leadership, business acumen,** and unwavering commitment to people development. These aren't just trophies on a shelf—they're the result of consistent, intentional effort to lead with excellence and empower others.

In 2011, James was inducted into the **Circle of Stars**, an elite recognition reserved for top-performing leaders within a Fortune 100 company. That same year, he achieved a rare trifecta of honors: **Outstanding Achievement, Making a Difference**, and **Community Impact** awards—each acknowledging his ability to not only drive results but uplift people and communities in the process.

These weren't one-time victories. In 2017 and 2018, under his leadership, companies experienced **record-breaking growth and operational success**, earning additional industry-wide recognition. These milestones weren't just business wins—they were reflections of the leadership systems, team cultures, and strategic clarity James had put into motion.

James doesn't chase awards. He chases **impact**—and the awards follow.

A Passion for Teaching and Coaching Leaders

More than anything, James is passionate about helping others become leaders.

Whether it's a high-potential employee in a struggling restaurant, a business owner looking to scale, or a corporate executive facing burnout, James approaches each coaching opportunity with the same belief: **"There is greatness inside of you—you just need the right tools, mindset, and accountability to unlock it."**

As a coach and leadership developer, James combines his personal story, the teachings of John C. Maxwell, and over 30 years of hands-on experience to guide people through a structured transformation. His programs are designed to deliver more than inspiration—they produce real, measurable change.

His coaching focuses on:

- **Self-awareness and emotional intelligence**

- **Leadership mindset and identity**

- **Team development and culture-building**

- **Strategic thinking and execution**

- **Accountability systems that sustain growth**

He has personally mentored hundreds of leaders across industries, helping them elevate their performance, transform team dynamics, and most importantly—**lead with purpose and integrity**.

CEO of Mika Restaurants: A Story of Transformation

In 2020, James stepped into his biggest turnaround challenge yet: taking over a failing restaurant brand on the brink of bankruptcy.

Mika Restaurants was struggling—burdened with debt, plagued by low morale, and barely surviving with two locations. Many believed the business was finished. James saw an opportunity.

As **CEO**, he didn't just restructure operations—he rebuilt the vision. He redefined the company's identity, empowered his team, and turned Mika into one of **Panama's fastest-growing restaurant franchises**.

Within five years, Mika expanded from **two to seven thriving locations**, earning multiple awards and a reputation for excellence in both service and food quality. What was once a forgotten brand is now a **national success story**, serving as the official cafeteria provider for the **employees of the Panama Canal**—a monumental achievement and a testament to what visionary leadership can do.

Mika's transformation was about more than food. It was about:

- **Building a winning culture**

- **Empowering local talent**
- **Implementing systems that scale**
- **Creating experiences that customers love and employees are proud of**

The success of Mika isn't just measured in profit. It's measured in people—those who now believe in their potential, in what's possible, because they were part of something bigger.

Before We Begin: A Word from James

James often says that **leadership is influence**—not a title, not a position, but the ability to inspire and empower others toward a shared goal. His mission is clear: to continue helping individuals and organizations **transform through intentional leadership development, mindset mastery, and strategic action.**

"The most fulfilling thing I've ever done is help others discover their potential and evolve into true leaders. When you transform into a leader, it changes every part of your life—**personally and professionally.** It gives you clarity, direction, and the power to impact others."

"This process isn't easy. You will stumble. You will fail. But those failures will become your greatest teachers. They'll force you to hold up the mirror, examine who you are, and make the hard changes. That's when growth begins. That's when real leadership is born."

James doesn't just love leadership—**he lives it**. Every conversation, every keynote, every workshop, every consulting session is driven by one goal: to **add value and activate growth.**

In this book, you'll discover the **10 Keys to Leadership** that have helped James—and so many others—transform their mindset, their teams, and their lives. These principles aren't theories. They're lived truths, born in the streets of East Harlem, sharpened in the U.S. Coast Guard, tested in boardrooms, and proven in businesses around the world.

Whether you're a frontline employee, a rising manager, an entrepreneur, or a corporate executive, Leadership Unlocked will Open the Keys to Leadership for you. With the right mindset, the right strategies, and the right mentor—**anything is possible.**

Chapter 2

The Key of the Mirror

"The mirror reflects what you see, but only you can define what it means." – Unknown

Leadership doesn't begin with a title, a promotion, or a corner office—it begins with you. Before you can effectively lead others, you must first learn to lead yourself. And that journey starts with the Key of the Mirror.

The mirror is symbolic. It forces us to pause, reflect, and confront who we truly are—not just who we hope others see. It doesn't just show the surface; it reveals the hidden truths we often ignore. This key demands courage—the courage to face our flaws, acknowledge our patterns, and commit to growth.

It asks you powerful questions: Where are you in your personal and professional journey? What are your true strengths, your blind spots, and the areas you know you've been avoiding? Are you leading from purpose or performance? From authenticity or appearance?

The Key of the Mirror is the foundation of transformational leadership because it builds the inner clarity required to create external impact. Without it, your leadership is based on tactics. With it, your leadership is driven by truth.

Everything you build—your culture, your results, your relationships—will ultimately reflect who you are on the inside. And the mirror will always be there, waiting for you to look—not with judgment, but with responsibility. Because the leader you become tomorrow is shaped by the reflection you're willing to face today.

The mirror is symbolic. It forces us to pause, reflect, and confront who we truly are—not just who we hope others see. This key asks: Where are you in your personal and professional journey? What are your true strengths, your blind spots, and the areas you know you've been avoiding?

Early Lessons in Leadership

Early in my career, I believed leadership was about authority—directing people, managing tasks, being in charge. But over time, I discovered a deeper truth: the most effective leaders start by mastering themselves.

One defining moment came during my transition from being a manager to a true leader. I realized that while I could control schedules and operations, I couldn't ignite passion or loyalty in others without first understanding who I was, what I valued, and how I showed up every day.

In the U.S.Coast Guard, I was pushed into situations that tested me—not just technically, but emotionally and mentally. Leading a crew under pressure taught me a powerful lesson: self-doubt clouds judgment, but self-awareness sharpens it. The more I understood myself—my triggers, my limitations, my internal dialogue—the better I became at responding with clarity and confidence.

Refining Leadership in the Corporate World

Those early lessons followed me into the corporate arena, where the stakes were higher and the challenges more complex. In this environment, leadership wasn't just about executing tasks—it was about influencing outcomes, managing diverse teams, and fostering a culture that aligned with both performance and purpose.

While managing one of the leading restaurant brand's highest-performing locations, I applied what I had learned: leadership begins within. I made it my mission to become the most self-aware person in the room—not to dominate, but to lead with clarity. I observed how my energy affected the team, how my tone influenced communication, and how my presence could either inspire or discourage.

That internal focus began to produce external results. My commitment to personal growth allowed me to coach team members more effectively, anticipate breakdowns before they occurred, and make decisions that were both strategic and empathetic. We didn't just hit goals—we shattered them. Customer satisfaction improved, employee turnover decreased, and we built a team culture that people didn't want to leave.

Later, as Regional Leader for a major energy company, I began implementing structured self-reflective practices with my management teams. I challenged them to examine their decisions and behaviors, not to find fault, but to uncover insights. That simple act—looking in the mirror—transformed performance, improved communication, and cultivated a culture of accountability and continuous improvement.

Learning Without a Mentor

When I first committed to becoming a better leader, I didn't have a mentor to guide me. I wasn't born into wealth or access. I had to seek knowledge like it was oxygen. I turned to books, tapes, audio programs, and any seminar I could find. I studied leadership classics during lunch breaks, listened to motivational speakers in my car, and attended workshops with pen and notepad in hand.

I created my own leadership curriculum. I built a habit of immersing myself in learning daily, even if it was just ten minutes at a time. I absorbed wisdom from authors like John C. Maxwell, Stephen Covey, Zig Ziglar, Les Brown, and Jim Rohn and many others. These voices became my early mentors. They challenged my thinking, helped shape my mindset, and modeled a level of personal responsibility that I wasn't seeing around me.

I learned to connect dots others didn't see. I'd hear a concept in a audio tape and try it on my team meeting the next day. I'd read a chapter on emotional intelligence and apply it to a difficult conversation with an employee. My growth wasn't theoretical—it was lived, practiced, and tested in real-time.

Most importantly, I learned to be teachable. No matter how much I thought I knew, I remained hungry. That hunger opened doors. When I walked into rooms of seasoned professionals, I didn't pretend to have it all figured out—I asked questions. And that willingness to learn drew people in. It earned me access to wisdom I would've missed had I tried to act like I had all the answers.

Those resources became my teachers. And they taught me two critical truths:

1. Growth is your personal responsibility.
2. Mentors are everywhere—if you're willing to be a student.

Today, I've earned the privilege of having mentors like John C. Maxwell, my Uncle Remi Acosta, and others who have added immeasurable value to my life. But that didn't happen by accident. It happened because I showed up for myself first. You don't wait for a mentor—you become someone worth mentoring.

The Mirror as a Tool for Growth

The mirror doesn't lie. It doesn't flatter. It reflects reality. But it also reveals opportunity. The key is what you do with what you see.

In my corporate journey, I stopped pointing fingers and started asking better questions. When something didn't go as planned, I learned to pause and ask, "What could I have done differently?" That shift—from blame to ownership—transformed not only my results, but also the culture around me. It made leadership less reactive and more intentional.

Over time, I developed a framework of personal review I called "Mirror Moments." These were structured pauses throughout the week where I would step back and evaluate the emotional, strategic, and relational impact of my leadership. Was I being clear or confusing? Empowering or micromanaging? These reflections allowed me to course-correct in real-time rather than waiting for things to fall apart.

I also began teaching my leadership teams how to build their own Mirror Moments. We incorporated it into one-on-ones and team meetings. Instead of just talking about metrics, we talked about mindset. We asked, "What part of this result was a reflection of us as leaders?" That one question sparked growth that spreadsheets could never measure.

Leadership is not about perfection. It's about progress through self-honesty. Every time you stand in front of that metaphorical mirror and own your actions, you grow stronger, clearer, and more equipped to lead others.

Practical Applications of the Key of the Mirror

If you want to unlock the Key of the Mirror in your own life, here are powerful ways to begin:

Start a Daily Reflection Practice Dedicate time at the end of each day to reflect. Journaling is a powerful tool to identify patterns in your thoughts and actions. Ask yourself:
1. What did I do well today?
2. Where did I miss the mark?
3. How can I improve tomorrow?

Seek FeedbackRegularly Feedback is often the mirror we avoid—but it's the one that tells the truth. Invite insights from trusted peers, team members, or mentors. Ask them:

1. How do I come across in meetings?
2. What's one thing I could do better as aleader?

Set PersonalGrowth Goals Choose one leadership trait to improve and work on it consistently.Struggle with delegation? Set a goal to delegate at least one meaningful task each week. Track your results and reflect on how it impacts your team.

UseSelf-Assessment Tools Instruments like the DISC Profile, Johari Window, or Emotional Intelligence surveys can provide valuable insight into your strengths and tendencies. Don't fear what they reveal—embrace the chance to grow.

Expanding Awareness Through Team Engagement

Self-awareness isn't just about you. It's about understanding how your leadership affects others.

As President of a hospitality company in Panama, I began facilitating team workshops focused on reflective practices. I invited my leaders to hold up the mirror—not just to themselves, but to how they were impacting their teams. The results were transformative.

In one case, a department head realized they were unknowingly creating confusion through vague communication. By recognizing the issue, they made deliberate changes—and within months, team collaboration improved and efficiency jumped by 20%.

That's the power of self-awareness: it improves you—and it multiplies through your people.

The Transformative Power of Self-Awareness

The Key of the Mirror is not a one-time practice. It's a lifelong leadership discipline. The moment you stop looking inward is the moment you start losing your edge. The best leaders reflect often.

They grow consistently. They remain honest with themselves—especially when no one else is watching.

Self-awareness is the foundation of emotional intelligence, and emotional intelligence is the backbone of influential leadership. When you know how you're wired—your default reactions, your fears, your internal motivators—you don't just lead by skill, you lead by presence. You become someone who can adapt under pressure, respond with calm in chaos, and see others with clarity.

Throughout my leadership journey, I've seen how self-awareness transforms not only individuals, but entire organizations. When a leader owns their energy, the culture follows. When a leader humbles themselves, accountability rises. When a leader consistently reflects, innovation emerges. Teams are more willing to speak up, take risks, and bring their full selves to the mission.

Self-awareness also empowers better decision-making. It helps you recognize when ego is leading the way versus vision. It teaches you to pause before reacting, and to choose a response that serves the greater good—not just your pride or impulse.

Most importantly, self-awareness creates connection. People follow leaders who are real. Who admit mistakes. Who ask for input. Who show up the same whether they're on stage or in a hallway conversation. Authenticity isn't a trait you're born with—it's a result of intentional self-awareness.

By embracing this key, you create a foundation of leadership that's not only effective—it's authentic. And authenticity inspires people. It builds trust. It makes people want to follow.

Key Takeaways

Embracing The Mirror for Authentic Leadership.

Leadership starts within. True leadership is born from self-awareness, not authority. Before you can influence others, you must first confront your own beliefs, behaviors, and blind spots.

The mirror reveals both truth and opportunity. When you reflect with courage, you see not just where you are—but where you can grow. Reflection is not about guilt; it's about clarity and transformation.

Self-awareness is a skill, not a personality trait. It can be developed through daily practices like journaling, feedback-seeking, and structured reflection(e.g., Mirror Moments).

Grow this a choice—and a responsibility. No one else can do the inner work for you. Leadership development isn't handed to you; it's owned by you. Leaders who reflect, learn.

Teachable leaders become magnetic. People are drawn to those who remain open, humble, and hungry to grow. Asking questions earns more trust than giving orders.

Feedback is your ally, not your enemy. When you seek input without defensiveness, you open doors to connection, collaboration, and innovation.

Self-aware leaders shape culture. How you show up as a leader influences the tone, trust, and trajectory of your organization. Your emotional presence is contagious.

Authenticity builds influence. Leaders who are honest about their imperfections and intentional about their growth inspire loyalty and respect. Being real is more powerful than being perfect.

The mirror is not a one-time check—it's a daily tool. Leadership isn't static. The best leaders keep looking inward, learning from yesterday, and adjusting for tomorrow.

By integrating these takeaways into your leadership practice, you don't just grow—you create a ripple effect that empowers others to do the same. The mirror doesn't show you who to become. It shows you where to begin.

Reflective Questions: Looking Into Your Leadership Mirror

1. When was the last time I paused to reflect on how I'm showing up as a leader?
2. What recurring patterns—positive or negative—do I notice in my leadership behaviors?
3. How do I typically respond to feedback? Do invite it regularly or avoid it?
4. What emotions tend to drive my decisions during moments of pressure or conflict?
5. In what areas of my leadership am I still wearing a mask or trying to impress rather than lead authentically?
6. How often do I check in with myself to align my leadership actions with my core values?
7. What do I want my leadership to *feel like* to the people I lead?
8. Where am I currently blaming others for outcomes I need to take more responsibility for?
9. What's one small daily habit I can adopt to become more self-aware and reflective?
10. If my team held up a mirror to my leadership today, what would they see—and how would I feel about it?

Mirror Moment Template

Date:_____

Leadership Context (Meeting / Decision / Challenge / Opportunity):

1. What Happened?

Briefly describe the situation, event, or moment you're reflecting on.

Example: Led a team meeting to address low morale.

2. How Did I Show Up?

1. What mindset or energy did I bring?
2. Was I calm, reactive, confident, distracted, open?

3. What Impact Did I Have?

1. How did others respond to me?
2. Did my words or actions move the situation forward or create confusion?

4. What Can I Learn From This?

1. What did I do well?
2. What would I do differently next time?

5. Leadership Check-In

Rate yourself 1–5 (1 = needs growth, 5 = excellent):

Leadership Trait ☐ Rating ☐ Clarity of Communication ☐ Emotional Presence ☐ Listening / Empathy ☐ Ownership & Accountability ☐ Alignment with My Values ☐

6. Next Step

What is one small action I will take to improve based on this reflection?

Example: Ask for anonymous feedback from my team after the next meeting.

Chapter 3

The Key of Self-Belief

"You become what you believe. You are where you are today in your life based on everything you have believed." – Oprah Winfrey

Leadership is built on many things—skill, strategy, vision—but without belief in yourself, none of it holds together. The Key of Self-Belief is the foundation that allows every other leadership trait to stand tall.

Before others believe in your vision, your message, or your direction, they must believe in *you*. And they will only believe in you to the extent that *you* believe in yourself. Confidence isn't arrogance. It's clarity. It's knowing who you are, what you stand for, and that your presence matters.

Where Belief Is Born
The Early Struggles of Confidence

There was a time when I wrestled deeply with self-belief. On the outside, I may have looked confident. But inside, I carried the weight of doubt—wondering if I was truly ready, capable, or enough.

One of those defining moments came when I was tasked with overseeing an international expansion for a U.S.-based restaurant group. It was one of my first major projects outside the country. The scope was massive, the expectations were sky-high, and I was stepping into uncharted waters—culturally, logistically, and operationally.

Did I feel fear? Absolutely. Did I let it define me? Absolutely not.

Instead, I dove headfirst into preparation. I immersed myself in learning—studying the local market, building trusted relationships, and absorbing everything I could from people who understood the landscape better than I did. I didn't wait to feel ready—I worked to become ready.

Knowledge replaced fear. Action replaced hesitation. And ultimately, the project became a success—not just in results, but in what it revealed to me about myself.

Self-belief isn't something you're born with. It's something you build. It doesn't arrive in a moment of inspiration—it's formed through pressure, persistence, and proof. For me, belief was born in adversity. It was forged in environments where I had to show up, even when I wasn't sure I was ready. I didn't wake up with confidence—I developed it through commitment.

In the Coast Guard, there was no time for doubt. Lives depended on decisions. One mission in particular stands out. We were operating under high stress, in dangerous waters, and the pressure to get it right was immense. I was young, still finding my footing, but I had to lead. I had to act. That moment taught me something I've never forgotten: courage is often doing the right thing before you feel ready. Belief came not from perfection, but from showing up, learning fast, and refusing to quit.

And not just once—but again and again. Repetition built resilience. Leadership became a rhythm of taking one more step, making one more decision, and trusting that with each challenge, I was becoming the leader I needed to be.

Later in the corporate world, belief grew as I learned to overcome my own internal resistance. That voice that whispered, "You're not ready," or "Who are you to lead?"—I had to confront it. I didn't silence it overnight. I responded with action. Every win, every challenge I pushed through, became another brick in the foundation of my self-belief.

Self-Belief vs. External Validation

The dangerous trap is confusing self-belief with approval. We live in a culture addicted to applause. Social media, performance reviews, public praise—these things can be helpful, but they can also become a crutch. When your identity is tied to applause, titles, or external wins, your leadership becomes fragile. It only works when the crowd is cheering.

Real self-belief doesn't need a stage—it lives in the quiet decisions no one sees. It shows up when no one is watching, when the stakes are high, and when there's no guarantee of recognition. It's in those moments that belief in yourself becomes either your anchor or your downfall.

I've seen leaders crumble after losing a position, receiving critical feedback, or missing a big goal—not because they weren't capable, but because their self-worth was rooted in achievement. That's the danger of relying on external validation: it builds a leadership identity on shifting sand.

When I was building Mika Café in Panama, belief wasn't based on whether people believed in *me*. It was built on knowing I had something valuable to offer. It came from my faith, my preparation, and my refusal to let fear be the loudest voice in the room. I had to lead without applause. I had to make decisions when the outcome was uncertain. And I had to find my own voice before anyone else could hear it.

Early in my leadership career, winning awards and receiving validation felt like everything. I measured my growth by the number of plaques on my wall or the applause in the room. It was intoxicating—but dangerous. At times, the attention inflated my ego more than it reinforced my self-belief. And that can be a risky combination—an inflated ego without a grounded identity. Ego whispers that you're more important than the mission. Self-belief reminds you that you're here to serve it.

Self-belief is internal fuel. External validation is just the echo. Great leaders know the difference—and they invest in the fuel first.

The Role of Faith and Vision

Self-belief is deeply tied to your sense of purpose. For me, my faith in God has always been a core driver. Even when I didn't feel capable, I knew I was called. That higher belief fueled my courage. Whether you connect with that through spirituality, a mission, or personal values, leaders must ground themselves in something *bigger* than their doubts.

Faith anchors you when results are shaky. It reminds you that you are more than what you've accomplished. There were seasons in my life—personally and professionally—where I didn't have external proof of success, but I had an internal promise. That's where faith takes over. It doesn't eliminate fear; it overpowers it.

When I entered Mika Café during the pandemic as President, I didn't have a roadmap. I had a vision. And that vision became the fuel. Vision is a form of belief that sees beyond what is and reaches for what could be. It allows you to take the next step without seeing the entire staircase. And the clearer the vision, the stronger the belief that follows.

Vision also keeps you moving when you feel stuck. It reminds you that your leadership isn't about this moment—it's about the movement you're building. Whether you're leading a family, a team, or an entire organization, your belief must be rooted in a vision bigger than yourself.

When you combine faith with vision, you don't just lead from skill—you lead from conviction. That's the kind of belief that inspires others to rise with you.

Building Self-Belief Practically

Self-belief grows when you create a rhythm of small, intentional actions that reinforce your worth, capability, and purpose. It's not just a mindset—it's a discipline. Here are some of the most effective ways I've found to build it:

1. **Track Your Wins:** Keep a record of successes—big or small. Review them often to remind yourself that you are capable. I kept a personal journal where I wrote down not just outcomes, but how I showed up with character, how I made tough decisions, and how I influenced others for good. Over time, this became a well of encouragement I could draw from when doubt tried to creep in.

2. **Affirm Your Identity:** Speak truth over yourself daily. Not hype, but affirmations rooted in your values and mission. Your words shape your world. Declare the leader you are becoming—not based on who you were, but who you are committed to be. I wrote mine on sticky notes and placed them on my bathroom mirror, dashboard, and desk.

3. **Act Despite Fear:** The fastest way to build belief is to act. Courage compounds. Every bold step confirms your identity as a leader. I can trace every leap in my leadership back to

a moment where I said yes to something that scared me. Action creates evidence—and evidence creates belief.

4. **Surround Yourself with Builders:** Spend time with people who speak to your strengths, challenge your excuses, and reflect your greatness back to you. These are your belief builders. Cut back on time with those who drain your energy or plant seeds of doubt. Your environment is shaping you more than you think.

5. **Reflect on What You've Overcome:** Your past victories—especially the quiet ones—are proof of your resilience and potential. Don't forget the moments where you made it through, even when no one was watching. Sometimes belief grows not by looking forward, but by remembering how far you've already come.

Belief Is Contagious

Teams don't just follow confident leaders—they are shaped by them. The energy of your belief becomes a silent permission slip for your team to believe in themselves. When a leader walks into the room fully grounded, that sense of security cascades through the organization. People become more willing to take initiative, to speak up, and to stretch beyond their comfort zones.

I've witnessed this firsthand in moments of uncertainty. When teams were unsure or overwhelmed, I learned that my steadiness became their confidence. Not because I had all the answers, but because I believed we could figure it out—together. That belief created a safety net for bold thinking.

Self-belief doesn't just affect performance—it affects culture. It fosters an environment where people don't just execute tasks—they

LEADERSHIP UNLOCKED: 10 KEYS TO INFLUENCE... 27

grow. They innovate. They rise. In that kind of atmosphere, people don't fear failure as much as they fear not trying.

The most powerful thing about contagious belief is that it multiplies. One leader with conviction can ignite an entire team. One act of courage can inspire others to rise. And one decision to lead from faith instead of fear can shift the culture of an entire organization.

Your self-belief isn't just for you—it's a leadership gift to everyone who follows you. Your certainty creates clarity. Your groundedness brings courage. Your vision unlocks theirs. That's the ripple effect of leadership fueled by belief.

Key Takeaways

The Power of Self-Belief in Leadership

Self-belief is not ego—it's alignment. It's the quiet power of knowing who you are and standing firm in your purpose, even when circumstances try to shake it. It allows you to lead with both humility and confidence, grounded in something deeper than applause.

Self-belief gives you the resilience to keep going when results don't come immediately, and the clarity to make decisions that reflect your mission—not your mood.

Great leaders don't just carry belief—they transmit it. They walk into the room and elevate it. They move through challenge with steady hands and speak vision that others can borrow.

Self-belief is a gift to others because it creates safety, energy, and trust. It's not about pretending you have it all figured out—it's about showing up anchored in who you are and who you're becoming.

Reflective Questions

1. Where in your leadership are you relying on external validation rather than internal belief?

2. What would it look like to act today as if you truly believed

in your value and purpose?

3. How has fear disguised itself as logic in your leadership decisions?

4. Who in your life reinforces your belief—and who drains it?

5. What past moment proves that you are more capable than you've given yourself credit for?

6. When have you mistaken ego for self-belief, and what was the impact?

7. How do you respond when belief is shaken—what anchors you in those moments?

8. What vision are you holding onto that gives your leadership meaning beyond today?

9. What's one action you can take this week to reinforce your belief in yourself through discipline, preparation, or reflection?

10. Who on your team could benefit from your belief in them—and how can you show it?

Self-Belief Mirror Moment Template
Date: _____ Leadership Moment/Context:
1. What challenge or moment tested my belief today?

    1. Did I hesitate, doubt myself, or play small? Why?

    2. Did I rise with confidence or shrink back in fear?

2. What belief did I lead with?

1. Was I anchored in purpose, or driven by approval?

   2. Did I act from conviction or reaction?

3. What inner voice dominated my thoughts?

   1. Was it faith, fear, ego, or clarity?

   2. How did it affect my leadership in the moment?

4. What did I learn about myself from this moment?

   1. Strengths I affirmed:

   2. Areas I need to strengthen:

5. Affirmation Check-In

Write a short affirmation to reconnect with your identity as a leader:

Example: "I lead from vision, not fear. I am called, prepared, and enough."

6. Commitment to Action

What small act of belief can I take tomorrow to lead from strength?

Example: Speak confidently in the next team meeting without downplaying my voice.

Chapter 4

The Key of Direction

> "It is not the wind, but the set of the sails, that determines the direction we will go." – Jim Rohn

A leader without direction is like a ship adrift at sea—vulnerable to every storm, every current, every distraction. Without a destination, even the most talented team will wander. The Key of Direction is about setting a clear course for yourself and your team, adjusting when needed, and staying focused through uncertainty and resistance.

Direction isn't just about having a plan. It's about having purpose, clarity, and alignment—and the courage to lead others toward something greater.

Setting the Course

Early in my leadership journey, I witnessed firsthand what happens when direction is missing. I worked with a growing organization in the hospitality sector that had potential—but lacked clarity. Leadership goals weren't aligned, team members were confused about their priorities, and morale was dropping fast.

There was no north star.

That experience stuck with me. It taught me that no matter how much talent exists within an organization, without vision and direction, people will operate in silos, energy will be wasted, and results will suffer.

Years later, when I became Vice President of Operations for an international restaurant group, I was given the responsibility of launching a major U.S. restaurant brand into a new Latin American market. The brand was unknown in the region, and local teams were unsure how to connect with the concept.

I knew our success would depend on more than just logistics—it would require a crystal-clear vision and a team-wide understanding of the direction we were headed. I broke down the vision into milestones, built performance benchmarks, and communicated expectations across every department. Every team member—from kitchen prep to senior leadership—understood their role in the mission.

The result? The most successful international opening in the company's history.

Adapting to Change

But direction is not rigidity. Leadership also demands flexibility. The wind will change—you have to know when to adjust the sails. It's not about abandoning the mission; it's about having the wisdom to shift your method without losing momentum.

During the height of the COVID-19 pandemic, I was leading a growing café brand in Central America. Practically overnight, customer behavior shifted, regulations changed, and the supply chain collapsed in ways we never anticipated. We couldn't operate as we had before—everything had to be reevaluated.

At first, the pressure was overwhelming. There were moments where fear crept in—not just for the business, but for the people who depended on it. But I knew panic wouldn't solve the problem—clarity would. I gathered my leadership team and together, we assessed the new reality. We didn't just ask what had changed—we asked what we could change.

We pivoted operations to focus on delivery and takeout. We created new protocols that ensured safety while maintaining service excellence. We also redefined team roles, making sure every person felt essential to the new mission. Every single adjustment we made was tied back to our original vision—we weren't just reacting, we were evolving.

What amazed me most was how the adversity revealed strengths we hadn't seen before. Team members stepped up. Creativity surged. Morale actually improved because we weren't just surviving—we were adapting with purpose.

That adaptability didn't just save the business—it strengthened our culture. It taught us that when direction is rooted in purpose, it doesn't crumble under pressure. It bends. It recalibrates. And it comes back stronger.

Involving Your Team in the Vision

One of the greatest lessons I've learned is this: Direction is most powerful when it's shared.

During my time as a regional leader in the energy sector, I developed collaborative planning sessions that brought managers into the strategic process. We built regional visions together—one store at a time. When people are involved in setting the course, they don't just comply—they commit. They show up differently. They take ownership.

But it's more than involvement—it's investment. When your team feels like co-creators of the vision, they become emotionally attached to it. They begin to see the success of the organization as a reflection of their own purpose. That's when you start to see a shift: from employees to leaders, from task managers to mission carriers.

I remember leading a multi-unit strategy meeting with a team that had been experiencing division between locations. Instead of dictating the new plan, I brought everyone together and asked a simple question: "What do we want to build together?" That opened a conversation that created clarity, unity, and commitment at every level. It also revealed solutions I hadn't considered—because those closest to the work often have the most practical insight.

When teams feel connected to the vision, they go from passengers to co-navigators. They don't just work toward goals—they drive them. And that shift—from compliance to co-creation—is what transforms direction from a strategy into a movement.

Practical Tools for Establishing Direction

Great leaders don't just talk about vision—they make it visible, measurable, and achievable. They translate dreams into daily action and direction into culture. Here are practical tools and strategies to help you bring direction to life for yourself and your team:

1. Vision Mapping – Don't just keep the vision in your head—put it on paper. Break it down into short-term (30/60/90-day) and long-term (1–3 years) objectives using bullet points, flowcharts, or mind maps. A vision map gives you and your team a tangible target and roadmap for action.

2. Milestone Meetings – Schedule regular check-ins (weekly,

monthly, quarterly) to evaluate progress, celebrate wins, and adjust direction as needed. These meetings keep your team mission-centered and momentum-driven. It also prevents drift and realigns energy with purpose.

3. Performance Dashboards – Use visual tracking tools to make progress visible. Dashboards allow everyone to see key metrics, goals, and milestone achievements in real-time. They promote transparency, drive accountability, and foster a sense of shared ownership.

4. Team Vision Workshops – Invite your team to co-create the path forward. Host workshops where members contribute to shaping the vision, defining roles, and aligning priorities. When people are part of the process, they're more engaged, more committed, and more likely to follow through.

5. Mission Alignment Tools – Use structured frameworks like V2MOM (Vision, Values, Methods, Obstacles, and Measures) or OKRs (Objectives and Key Results) to ensure that daily tasks align with your long-term vision and organizational values. These tools bridge the gap between strategy and execution.

6. Daily and Weekly Intentions – Start each day or week with intention-setting. Use team huddles or personal journaling to clarify priorities and focus. End the week with reflection: What worked? What needs adjusting? These rituals build rhythm and realignment into your leadership habits.

7. Visual Reinforcement – Make vision unavoidable. Use posters, digital screens, mission statement walls, or creative

signage to reinforce key values and objectives in the workplace. When vision is seen consistently, it stays top of mind and becomes embedded in the culture.

Each of these tools is a way to turn direction into daily momentum. By building these into your systems, routines, and leadership rhythm, you move from talking about vision to living it—and helping your team do the same.

Communicating Direction Effectively

Clarity of vision means nothing without clarity of communication. As a leader, your words shape direction—and culture.

When launching new restaurant concepts, I always began with vision alignment meetings. But I didn't stop there. I reinforced the direction in daily huddles, team check-ins, visual dashboards, and follow-up emails.

Here are strategies to communicate vision with clarity:

1. Start with the "Why" – Purpose fuels belief. Make the mission matter.

2. Use Storytelling – People remember stories more than bullet points.

3. Repeat Relentlessly – Consistency drives clarity. Say it often.

4. Make it Visual – Use visual aids to reinforce the message.

5. Customize Your Message – Tailor vision by audience. Speak their language.

6. Invite Dialogue – Create space for feedback and ownership.

7. Celebrate Alignment – Praise those who live the mission.

8. Lead by Example – Walk the talk. You are the vision's greatest ambassador.

Common Pitfalls of Direction—and How to Avoid Them

Even strong leaders fall into traps when it comes to establishing and maintaining direction. These missteps can stall progress, create confusion, and dilute impact. Here's a breakdown of common leadership pitfalls related to direction—and how to course-correct:

1. Ambiguity – A vague or overly complex vision creates confusion and stalls execution. Fix: Use clear, direct language. A vision should be so simple that everyone on your team can repeat it and apply it to daily decisions. Avoid jargon and get to the heart of what truly matters.

2. Rigidity – Refusing to adapt your strategy when circumstances change can derail your vision. Fix: Stay flexible in how you reach your goals. Maintain consistency in your purpose, but be agile in your methods. Build regular check-ins to reassess and adapt your path without losing sight of the destination.

3. Exclusion – Leaders who develop vision in isolation often miss buy-in and practical insight from the front lines. Fix: Involve key voices at every level—especially those closest to the customer or the process. Inclusion strengthens alignment and ownership.

4. Overcomplication – Leaders sometimes mistake complexity for depth, which results in paralysis. Fix: Keep it simple. Focus on 2–3 core priorities that directly move the vision for-

ward. Strip away distractions and communicate with clarity and focus.

5. Stagnation – A vision that's never revisited can become outdated or irrelevant. Fix: Schedule quarterly vision reviews and strategic resets. Encourage feedback on how the direction is playing out on the ground. Keep the mission fresh by linking it to real-time challenges and successes.

6. Lack of Reinforcement – Even the clearest direction will fade without regular reinforcement. Fix: Make vision a daily habit. Share stories of alignment, recognize values-based behavior, and integrate vision language into meetings, training, and celebrations.

Avoiding these pitfalls is not about perfection—it's about practicing awareness and leadership maturity. Direction is not just something you set once; it's something you steward daily. When you lead with clarity, flexibility, and inclusion, your direction becomes more than a statement—it becomes a culture.

Real-Life Success Stories

At one point while leading a fast-casual restaurant brand, I introduced a quarterly goal-setting system that involved everyone—from front-line employees to department heads. The outcome? Better performance, unity, and stronger culture. It wasn't just about hitting goals—it was about giving every person a voice in where we were going and how we'd get there. Because people commit more deeply to what they help create.

In another role developing international restaurants, I worked closely with local leaders to adapt the brand's direction to fit cultural norms. Their input prevented costly missteps and led to lasting success. We learned quickly that what worked in one market might alienate customers in another. By leaning into local wisdom and letting teams tailor strategies while staying rooted in brand values, we built something sustainable.

Another powerful example came when I was asked to step in and stabilize a struggling region for a national restaurant chain. The team was demoralized, turnover was high, and customer satisfaction was dropping. I didn't walk in with a new policy—I walked in with questions. I spent time listening to every layer of the operation. Then, together, we created a shared vision for what the region could become.

We aligned roles, redesigned processes, and created a rhythm of intentional leadership communication. Within six months, performance metrics improved by over 30%, and more importantly—the team believed in the mission again. That's the power of direction: when it's clear, shared, and owned, it creates momentum no incentive plan ever could.

Conclusion

The Key of Direction is not just about setting a goal—it's about creating a vision people believe in, adjusting with wisdom, and moving forward with purpose.

A leader with direction isn't afraid of storms. They know how to adjust the sails. They trust their crew. And they keep moving forward—always.

But let me be clear: the direction you're headed—your North Star—is sacred. It represents your purpose, your mission, and your why. That said, how you get there may change. You will face obstacles—economic downturns, physical challenges, unexpected disasters, or personal losses. That's part of the journey.

Leadership is not about rigidly holding onto one path. It's about being flexible and wise enough to reroute without losing sight of your ultimate destination. When the storm comes, don't abandon the mission—adjust your sails.

Great leaders stay focused on the vision while staying grounded in reality. That's how direction becomes more than just a compass—it becomes your anchor in chaos and your engine in progress.

And sometimes, direction means starting over. It may mean letting go of what no longer serves the mission. It may require closing a chapter, walking away from a plan that once felt right, or launching something entirely new. Starting over isn't failure—it's clarity in action. It's the courage to say, "This isn't the path anymore, but the destination still matters." That kind of leadership—the willingness to reset the sails and start again—builds not just organizations, but legacies.

Key Takeaways

The Power of Directional Leadership

• Direction brings clarity. When leaders articulate a clear path, it eliminates confusion and creates alignment across the team.

• Strong direction builds confidence. People perform better when they know where they're headed and how their role contributes to the vision.

• Vision must evolve. Direction is not static. Leaders must revisit, refine, and sometimes recalibrate the course to stay relevant and effective.

- Collaboration strengthens direction. Great leaders invite others to help shape the journey, creating shared ownership and increased engagement.
- Direction fuels resilience. When the path gets difficult, clarity of purpose helps teams stay grounded, focused, and motivated.
- Leadership requires adaptability. The goal may remain the same, but the route to get there must allow for agility, feedback, and innovation.
- Clear direction empowers transformation. Leaders who guide with purpose don't just manage—they inspire progress and activate potential.

Reflective Questions

1. Is your current direction anchored in a clear purpose—and have you communicated it in a way your team understands and connects with emotionally?

2. When challenges or unexpected changes arise, how prepared are you to adjust your strategy without compromising your vision?

3. What practical steps can you take to ensure your team is not just aware of the vision, but actively contributing to it and taking ownership of the outcome?

4. How consistently do you reinforce your direction through your communication, your culture, and your actions? What could you do more of?

5. If someone on your team were asked to describe the vision—would they say the same thing you would? If not, how can you bridge that gap?

6. In what ways are you creating space for your team to help shape the direction rather than just follow it?

7. Have you experienced a time when your direction needed to be reset or completely restarted? What did you learn from that experience?

8. Are there areas where you're holding onto a direction out of comfort or familiarity rather than alignment with your true mission?

9. How do you ensure your communication of direction is not only clear—but inspiring?

10. What tools or routines could you implement to keep direction top-of-mind for both yourself and your team?

Direction Mirror Moment Template

Date: _____ Leadership Context: _____

1. Where am I headed—and is it clear to me and my team?

1. Is our direction still aligned with our purpose?

2. Have I communicated it in a way that inspires and connects?

2. What signals suggest we need to adjust course?

1. Are there changes in the environment, results, or team dy-

namics?

   2. Am I holding onto an outdated plan out of comfort or ego?

3. How am I involving my team in shaping the direction?

   1. Are they contributors or just followers?

   2. What feedback or ideas have I invited lately?

4. Am I modeling the vision through my behavior and decisions?

   1. Do my daily actions reflect where we're going?

   2. What part of the vision have I embodied well? What needs work?

5. What needs to be restarted, simplified, or reinforced?

   1. Is there an area that needs a reset?

   2. Where can I remove confusion or increase clarity?

6. Next Step: What's one thing I can do this week to move us forward with clarity and purpose?

Example: Host a team vision check-in to realign and refresh our direction.

Chapter 5

The Key of Great Communication

"The art of communication is the language of leadership." – James Humes

Communication is the bridge that connects your leadership to your team, your vision to your execution, and your strategy to real results. It is not just a leadership skill—it is a leadership essential. Without great communication, even the best plans collapse under misunderstanding, misalignment, or mistrust.

Great communication isn't about having the perfect words—it's about creating authentic connections. It's about making sure your message is not only heard, but felt, understood, and acted upon. The most influential leaders I've met are not just charismatic speakers—they are empathetic listeners, intentional storytellers, and masters of presence. They speak with purpose and lead with clarity.

As you step into the Key of Great Communication, you'll explore how to build trust through clarity, deepen impact through empathy, and adapt your message for influence. Because in leadership, communication isn't part of the work—it is the work. The Key of Great Communication is about clarity, empathy, and adaptability—three elements that, when mastered, can elevate your influence, unify your team, and move your vision forward.

The Foundation of Communication

Communication is more than exchanging words—it's about creating understanding, connection, and momentum. In leadership, it becomes the invisible thread that ties people to purpose, aligns teams to goals, and sustains trust through pressure.

In the early stages of my leadership journey, I underestimated the power of communication. I believed giving instructions was enough. If I was clear, they would follow—or so I thought. But I learned quickly that true leadership is not a monologue—it's a dialogue. And if your people don't feel heard, they won't feel led.

When I stepped into the role of Vice President of Operations for a hospitality group in Latin America, I inherited a team that felt disconnected and disempowered. Productivity wasn't the issue—engagement was. There was talent in the room, but no emotional buy-in.

One of the first things I did was initiate consistent leadership connection meetings—intentional sessions where I could communicate company goals, invite real-time feedback, and open the floor for honest dialogue. These meetings weren't just about delivering updates—they were about building relationships and reinforcing trust. They sent a clear message: "Your voice matters here."

Over time, I began to see transformation. Confusion was replaced by clarity. Disengagement gave way to ownership. Frustration turned into momentum. Because when people feel informed, included, and inspired, they become more than employees—they become ambassadors of the mission.

LEADERSHIP UNLOCKED: 10 KEYS TO INFLUENCE... 45

That experience taught me a foundational truth: communication is not just a leadership tool—it is a leadership culture. And it starts with how you show up every day.

Tailoring Communication to Your Audience

A great communicator understands that one message does not fit all. Context matters. Culture matters. People matter.

While leading the expansion of a U.S. brand into Central America, I learned how vital it was to adapt my communication style. In Panama, relationship-driven dialogue was key—people responded best to warm, personal interactions. In Colombia, structure and professionalism carried more weight. One message delivered the same way in both places would have missed the mark in at least one.

This taught me a critical leadership lesson: effective communication is not just about what you say—it's about how it lands. And how it lands depends on how well you understand the person, the moment, and the mission.

I began asking myself before every important message: Who am I speaking to? What matters most to them? What is the emotional and cultural context behind this conversation? That shift made me not just more effective—but more respected.

Whether you're leading in a diverse global market or managing a small local team, tailoring your communication fosters inclusion, builds trust, and drives engagement. When people feel spoken with instead of spoken to, their response changes. Their energy shifts. Their contribution multiplies.

Practical Application:
1. Audience Assessment: Evaluate the team's cultural, emotional, and professional context. Ask yourself: "What mat-

ters to them right now?"

2. Adaptability: Adjust your tone, message, and delivery method to resonate more effectively. Formal or informal? Data-driven or story-based? Face-to-face or written?

3. Feedback Mechanisms: Encourage response, dialogue, and questions to ensure the message is truly received. Listening completes the communication loop.

The Art of Listening

Communication doesn't start with your voice—it starts with your ears.

Great leaders aren't just great speakers—they're exceptional listeners. They understand that communication is a two-way street, and that real connection happens when people feel heard, not just spoken to. Active listening is the gateway to trust, respect, and engagement. It's how you uncover what's truly happening beneath the surface.

During my time working in the retail and fuel sector, I implemented an open-door policy that wasn't just symbolic—it was functional. I made it a habit to invite feedback at every level of the organization. From front-line staff to senior managers, I asked questions that mattered: "What's working for you?" "What's getting in your way?" "What do you need from me to lead better?"

The responses were honest—and sometimes hard to hear. But that honesty was a gift. It gave me insight I wouldn't have gained from reports or dashboards. It helped me solve real problems, recognize blind spots, and strengthen trust across the team. As a result, we didn't just improve operations—we increased innovation and saw a measurable 13% rise in merchandise sales.

True listening is more than being silent while others speak. It's about being present. It's about setting aside your internal agenda to fully absorb what someone else is expressing—verbally and nonverbally. When people feel heard, they feel valued. And when they feel valued, they give their best.

To practice active listening:

1. Make eye contact and eliminate distractions. Be fully present.

2. Summarize or repeat back what you've heard to confirm understanding.

3. Ask clarifying questions that show curiosity, care, and respect.

4. Resist the urge to respond too quickly—pause, reflect, then reply.

Listening earns trust. Trust earns commitment. And commitment is the currency of great leadership.

Using Technology to Enhance Communication

In today's world, communication must evolve with technology. The pace, platforms, and preferences of your team are constantly changing—and as a leader, you must be ready to meet them where they are.

During one of the most disruptive seasons of my leadership—while running a restaurant group during the COVID-19 pandemic—I leaned heavily on video conferencing, shared dashboards, and instant messaging platforms to keep communication seamless. These tools weren't just convenient—they were critical to survival and success.

But the evolution hasn't stopped there. Today, artificial intelligence (AI) is also emerging as a powerful communication enhancer. AI-driven platforms can analyze team sentiment, summarize meetings, and even personalize internal communications based on behavior patterns and roles. Used strategically, AI can help leaders become more responsive, informed, and effective.

That said, technology should never replace human connection—but when used wisely, it enhances it. Great leaders use tools to amplify their presence, not replace it. Whether through a well-timed team video message, a shared project tracker, or an AI-generated report that helps you better understand employee engagement, the goal is the same: stronger, faster, more authentic communication.

Strategies:

1. Use project management platforms for visibility and accountability.

2. Use messaging apps for day-to-day coordination and morale.

3. Use video for connection—because body language still matters.

4. Explore AI tools that enhance understanding, automate feedback loops, and support team clarity.

Handling Difficult Conversations

Every leader, no matter how skilled, must face uncomfortable conversations. These are the moments that reveal the depth of your character, your ability to manage emotions, and your commitment to growth—not just for yourself, but for others. What defines great leadership is how we handle these moments—with honesty, empathy, and courage.

I once had to sit down with a senior leader whose management style was clashing with the company culture. There were complaints from his team about harsh tone, lack of recognition, and emotional disconnection. Instead of reacting out of frustration or defensiveness, I created a space for openness and accountability. I began the conversation by acknowledging his contributions, then invited him to see the gap between intention and impact. We didn't just talk about behavior—we discussed values, expectations, and the future of his leadership.

The result wasn't just a resolution—it was a transformation. He not only changed his approach, but he became a mentor to others on how to lead with empathy. That moment reminded me that difficult conversations aren't obstacles—they are doorways. When handled with skill, they create breakthrough.

Steps for Difficult Conversations:

1. Prepare: Be clear on the facts, desired outcome, and tone you want to set.

2. Choose the Right Setting: Private, neutral, and emotionally safe.

3. Use Empathy: Begin by acknowledging the other person's experience and intent.

4. Be Direct Yet Respectful: Speak with clarity, not avoidance.

5. Be Solution-Oriented: Focus on what's possible moving for-

ward, not just what went wrong.

Difficult conversations are unavoidable—but they're also a leadership gift. They shape culture, deepen trust, and unlock growth—for everyone involved.

Nonverbal Communication

People will remember how you made them feel—often more than what you said.

Your tone, facial expression, and body language either reinforce your message or contradict it. During team meetings or presentations, I always pay attention to posture, presence, and energy. Leadership is a performance—not to entertain, but to connect.

And this connection can be strengthened or shattered in the subtlest of moments. When someone—whether they report to you or not—shares their thoughts, concerns, or feelings, your facial expressions matter deeply. A smirk, an eye roll, or a dismissive look can instantly shut someone down. It sends the message: "Your voice doesn't matter here."

If you want to be a trusted communicator, you must communicate respect not just with your words—but with your presence. Your face, your eyes, and your posture all speak. Make sure they are saying what you intend.

Tips for Effective Nonverbal Communication:

1. Maintain an open and confident stance.

2. Use eye contact to convey respect.

3. Let your tone match your message—calm, passionate, serious, or celebratory as needed.

4. Check your facial expression when listening—especially during moments of disagreement or vulnerability.

Words may speak—but energy convinces.

Building a Communication Culture

Great communication isn't a task—it's a culture. And it starts at the top. Leaders set the tone for how information flows, how feedback is received, and how voices are valued. A culture of communication is one where clarity is prioritized, listening is practiced, and transparency is modeled every day—not just during meetings or when things go wrong.

While leading a restaurant and hospitality expansion, I introduced a communication development program for all leadership levels. We focused on transparent messaging, proactive listening, and building emotional intelligence. The shift in morale was visible—and it directly impacted customer service and team performance during one of our most successful openings.

But building this culture required more than training—it required consistency. We integrated communication practices into our onboarding, leadership evaluations, and team rituals. Daily huddles included space for input. Monthly reviews emphasized not just performance but communication strengths and opportunities. We celebrated people not only for what they accomplished—but how they kept others informed and inspired along the way.

And at the core of all of it was emotional maturity. A culture of great communication can only be built by leaders who are self-aware, secure, and emotionally grounded. It takes humility to admit when communication has broken down, empathy to hear feedback without defensiveness, and wisdom to know when to speak, when to listen, and when to pause. Communication culture is not sustained by charisma—it is sustained by character.

A strong communication culture ensures that no one feels invisible, misunderstood, or left out of the loop. It increases psychological safety and encourages people to speak up—about risks, concerns, and innovative ideas. Over time, it becomes the heartbeat of high-performing teams.

Actionable Steps:

1. Offer regular communication training.

2. Use internal newsletters or videos to keep the message alive.

3. Celebrate great communicators on your team.

4. Lead by example—speak clearly, listen often, and stay connected.

5. Integrate communication into leadership reviews and team rituals.

6. Make space in every meeting for reflection and two-way feedback.

Conclusion

The Key of Great Communication is not just about talking—it's about connecting.

It's the bridge between vision and execution, between leadership and followership. When done well, communication inspires. It unifies. It resolves. It transforms.

If you want to build strong teams, foster accountability, and move people toward a shared goal—start by becoming a great communicator. Learn to listen deeply, speak intentionally, and connect consistently.

But more than anything, understand this: communication is a leadership responsibility that never turns off. It shows up in every gesture, every tone, every meeting, every silence. Your ability to lead is directly connected to your ability to communicate—not just down the chain, but across and upward too. People don't just follow words—they follow energy, consistency, and integrity.

It's not about being perfect—it's about being present. It's about having the emotional maturity to handle hard conversations with grace, the clarity to align teams with vision, and the humility to listen more than you speak.

Great communicators don't just deliver messages—they build bridges of trust. They transform tension into truth, confusion into clarity, and ideas into action. That's what makes communication not just a leadership tool—but one of its most transformational keys.

Because in leadership, your message is not just what you say—it's what they hear, feel, and believe.

Key Takeaway

Great communication is the cornerstone of effective leadership.

Practice it with intention and humility. Speak with clarity. Listen with purpose. Adapt with emotional intelligence.

Communication is more than a skill—it's a leadership mindset. When leaders communicate with empathy and authenticity, they create trust, alignment, and resilience in their teams. Every word, gesture, and silence sends a message—make sure it's one of respect, connection, and clarity.

In high-pressure moments, great communication is what steadies the team. In uncertainty, it becomes the anchor. When you cultivate a culture of communication—rooted in emotional maturity, trust, and consistency—you create space where people feel safe to contribute, challenge, and grow.

When communication becomes part of your leadership DNA, you don't just inform—you inspire. You don't just direct—you empower. And that's when transformation begins.

Reflective Questions

1. Are you speaking in a way that connects with your team emotionally, or are you simply relaying information?

2. How intentionally do you adjust your communication style to align with the cultural, emotional, or contextual needs of your audience?

3. Are you listening to understand or listening to respond? What can you do to deepen your active listening practice?

4. How effectively are you using technology and AI to reinforce connection, collaboration, and clarity?

5. Do your tone, energy, and nonverbal cues reflect the level of respect and maturity you expect from your team?

6. When was the last time you had a difficult conversation that led to transformation? What did you learn about your communication style in that moment?

7. How are you helping to build a culture where communication is consistent, safe, and encouraged across every level of your team?

8. Where might emotional immaturity be limiting your communication impact—and how can you address it with growth and accountability?

Great Communication Mirror Moment Template

Date: _____ Leadership Context or Situation:

1. What communication moment stood out to me today?

1. Was it a success, a breakdown, or a moment of growth?

2. How did I show up in that moment—verbally and nonverbally?

2. How well did I listen?

1. Did I listen actively and without distraction?

2. Did I create space for others to speak freely?

3. Did I adapt my message to meet the needs of my audience?

1. Was I mindful of tone, timing, and delivery?

2. Did I consider the emotional or cultural context?

4. What did my body language and energy communicate?

1. Did I unintentionally dismiss or shut someone down with my expression or tone?

2. Did I communicate respect and openness?

5. Was there a difficult conversation I avoided, mishandled, or handled well? Why?

1. What can I learn from how I approached that moment?

6. How am I modeling a communication culture for my team?

1. Am I reinforcing psychological safety, feedback, and clarity?

2. Am I practicing emotional maturity in my daily leadership?

7. Affirmation:

Example: "My words carry weight, and my presence builds trust. I choose to lead through clarity, empathy, and truth."

Chapter 6

The Key of Follow up

"Success is in the follow-up. Consistency builds trust and results." – Unknown

Each of the other keys to leadership—Self-Awareness, Self-Belief, Direction, Communication, and those still to come—are powerful on their own. But without Follow-Up, none of them can perform at their highest level.

You can cast a bold vision, communicate it clearly, build belief, and set the right course—but if there's no follow-up, progress stalls. Follow-up is what transforms principles into performance. It's where leadership moves from words to action, from intention to implementation.

It's the engine that drives consistency, accountability, and results. And when practiced with discipline, it creates momentum that compounds over time—not just in projects, but in people.

The Importance of Follow-Up

Follow-up is the glue that holds a leader's entire framework together. Without it, Self-Awareness doesn't lead to growth, Self-Belief doesn't lead to courage, Direction doesn't lead to execution, and Communication doesn't lead to alignment. Follow-up connects every other key to real-world results. It is the daily discipline that turns vision into traction, and strategy into action.

Many leaders struggle not because they lack direction or intention, but because they fail to close the loop. Follow-up is that loop. It is the invisible structure that sustains forward movement—it creates clarity, accountability, and emotional safety. When people know that someone is checking in—not to control, but to support—they stay more focused and engaged.

Early in my leadership career as a regional director in the retail and energy sector, I was assigned to an underperforming territory. Morale was low, systems were broken, and results were flatlining. My first move? I implemented a system of consistent follow-up—not to micromanage, but to reconnect every person to the bigger picture. I set expectations clearly, checked in regularly, and supported each manager with tools and feedback. Within months, that region became one of the top performers.

It wasn't magic. It was consistent, intentional follow-up. It showed the team that leadership wasn't just watching—it was invested. And perhaps more importantly, it reminded people of what they were capable of. Follow-up isn't just operational—it's motivational. It tells your team: "I believe in what we're doing—and I believe in you."

Developing a Follow-Up System

A clear vision (Direction) and a strong belief in your team (Self-Belief) are important—but without structure, they're vulnerable to distraction and delay. That's where follow-up systems come in.

Follow-up systems create rhythm, accountability, and alignment. They don't have to be complex—but they do have to be intentional. A good follow-up system answers the questions: Who is doing what? By when? And how will we know it's complete?

In one of my hospitality leadership roles, I introduced a simple yet powerful task tracking system. This wasn't about control—it was about clarity. It helped ensure that our goals (set during planning and communication sessions) stayed front and center. The system included:

1. Task Assignments: Every person knew what they were responsible for. No assumptions.

2. Deadlines: Clear timelines gave structure and created urgency.

3. Progress Updates: Weekly status reports kept communication open and issues visible.

But we didn't stop there. We reviewed these updates together. We created space to discuss roadblocks and realign priorities. This turned the system into more than a checklist—it became a leadership tool for coaching, support, and culture building.

The key wasn't just following up on tasks—it was following up on people. Checking in on how they felt about their work, whether they had what they needed to succeed, and how aligned they felt with the mission. That's the real heart of a follow-up system: keeping your people connected to purpose, progress, and each other.

This system helped reduce operational inefficiencies, improved team responsiveness, and gave every team member the confidence to own their responsibilities—and deliver.

The Role of Communication in Follow-Up

You can't have effective follow-up without clear, ongoing communication. Communication gives your follow-up context, tone, and intention. It shifts follow-up from feeling like a checklist to becoming a collaborative, motivational experience.

I hold regular one-on-one check-ins with team members to discuss progress—not just on performance, but on mindset, challenges, and alignment. These follow-ups are where the real power of Communication meets action. It's a space to:

1. Celebrate wins: Recognition fuels motivation.

2. Identify challenges: Early detection means early solutions.

3. Offer support: Whether it's resources, coaching, or encouragement, support keeps people moving forward.

But communication in follow-up isn't just about updates. It's about presence. When you communicate with clarity, empathy, and curiosity, you're telling your team, "I see you. I'm with you. Let's figure this out together."

Effective follow-up conversations aren't rigid or transactional—they're dynamic. Sometimes they're structured performance reviews. Other times, they're spontaneous check-ins. The key is showing up consistently and authentically, creating trust that builds over time.

It's also critical to be mindful of how you communicate. Your tone, timing, and body language matter. A follow-up delivered with frustration or sarcasm can shut someone down. But one delivered with belief and care can reignite commitment.

This kind of follow-up shifts the focus from "Did you do this?" to "How can I help you succeed?" And when that becomes the norm, communication becomes a catalyst for action—not a source of pressure.

Balancing Accountability and Autonomy

Follow-up should empower, not stifle. And it should never replace trust—it should reinforce it.

In a leadership role within the hospitality industry, I found success by giving managers full ownership of their outcomes—while still maintaining consistent alignment check-ins. This balance supported the key of Self-Awareness (by holding people accountable to reflect and adjust) and the key of Communication (by keeping the conversation open and honest).

But more than that, follow-up is a way of showing your people that you want them to succeed.

When you follow up consistently, you're not checking up—you're coaching forward. You help your team understand what's expected, keep them aligned with the bigger picture, and catch potential mistakes early—before they become costly. You teach them how to manage themselves by guiding them through the process of reflection, responsibility, and growth.

Over time, as people begin to understand their roles more deeply and take ownership of their responsibilities, you can begin to step back. That's when accountability turns into autonomy. And that's when you shift from manager to coach—someone who empowers, encourages, and equips, rather than controls.

Using Technology to Enhance Follow-Up

save the project—or worse, damage trust and allow failure to snowball. True leadership means having the courage to face what follow-up reveals and taking ownership of what needs to be adjusted.

The more your team sees follow-up as a tool for their success, the more they'll embrace it.

Creating a Culture of Follow-Up

Follow-up shouldn't be a personal habit—it should be a cultural norm. A strong follow-up culture doesn't just happen—it's modeled, nurtured, and reinforced by leadership. It's woven into the everyday practices of the organization, where accountability is shared and celebrated, and everyone understands that follow-up is part of how we work—not just something we do when things go wrong.

In one business I led, we implemented a weekly leadership rhythm: department heads reviewed their progress, shared best practices, and realigned on shared objectives. These sessions supported every leadership key: Communication, Direction, Responsibility, and more. But beyond the structure, we built a mindset: that follow-up wasn't about control—it was about commitment. A commitment to excellence, to alignment, and to each other.

Creating this kind of culture starts with emotional maturity at the top. Leaders must be willing to engage consistently, respond thoughtfully, and own their own follow-through. This maturity models how others should behave and creates a safe space where feedback isn't feared but welcomed. Without it, follow-up feels like inspection. With it, it becomes inspiration.

Steps to Build a Follow-Up Culture:

1. Lead by Example: Do what you say you'll do. Every time. Let your actions be the standard.

2. Equip Your Team: Provide training on how to manage tasks, follow through, and navigate challenges.

3. Celebrate Commitment: Publicly recognize those who follow through consistently—it reinforces that accountability is a value, not a task.

4. Make It Visible: Use shared tools and routines so follow-up is part of daily workflows, not a hidden task.

5. Talk About It Openly: Reinforce follow-up in team meetings, one-on-ones, and leadership reviews.

When follow-up becomes part of your team's identity, momentum becomes unstoppable—and results become inevitable.

The Ripple Effect of Follow-Up

Great follow-up doesn't just close gaps—it builds trust.

When your team sees that you follow through on what you say, they believe in your leadership. When they know that you'll check in, support them, and expect excellence—they step up. In one hospitality organization, our commitment to structured follow-up led to stronger employee retention, higher performance, and better customer satisfaction.

But the impact doesn't stop there. Follow-up also has a measurable effect on business outcomes. In revenue-generating organizations, consistent follow-up improves operational efficiency, accelerates project completion, reduces costly errors, and increases client satisfaction—all of which directly contribute to higher profits. It ensures that every task tied to a financial goal stays on track.

And in mission-driven or nonprofit organizations, follow-up creates the structure needed for exponential growth. It helps ensure that volunteer teams stay engaged, donors stay informed, and critical initiatives are completed with excellence. It reinforces the message that impact isn't just an idea—it's a disciplined, coordinated effort.

Follow-up communicates something deeper than direction: it says, "You matter. This matters. Let's win together." And when that message becomes a habit, organizations don't just survive—they scale.

Conclusion

The Key of Follow-Up is what activates every other leadership principle. It brings structure to Direction, deepens Communication, reinforces Self-Awareness, and sustains results through accountability. It's the practical engine that powers leadership philosophy into visible progress.

Without follow-up, leadership is just talk. With it, leadership becomes a force for transformation—in your culture, your team, and yourself.

But more than execution, follow-up is a reflection of your commitment. It shows that you're not just interested in results—you're invested in the process. It reminds your team that their work matters, their growth matters, and the mission matters.

Follow-up doesn't just impact people—it directly impacts performance. It increases retention, reduces rework, boosts collaboration, and drives revenue. Whether you lead a business, nonprofit, or community organization, consistent follow-up fuels long-term momentum and sustainable impact.

It's not about control—it's about connection. And when leaders follow up with purpose and presence, they elevate everyone around them.

Key Takeaways

Follow-up is the engine of progress and the heartbeat of leadership execution.

It's the discipline that holds every other leadership key together—transforming values into habits, strategy into traction, and words into results.

When practiced with consistency, clarity, and care, follow-up becomes a culture.

It motivates individuals, aligns teams, strengthens communication, and builds trust.

It empowers people to take ownership, fosters autonomy, and creates space for course correction before it's too late.

More than just checking boxes, great follow-up connects people to purpose.

It increases revenue, reduces operational waste, supports innovation, and scales both for-profit and nonprofit missions. Whether you're managing a business or leading a movement, follow-up is the practical leadership multiplier that drives long-term impact.

Done right, it's not about control—it's about connection, clarity, and momentum.

Reflective Questions

1. What personal systems or routines can you implement to consistently follow through on your commitments—and how do they align with your leadership values?

2. In what ways has your follow-up built (or damaged) trust with your team in the past? What lessons can you apply going

forward?

3. How can you ensure that follow-up becomes part of your team's culture, rather than something that depends only on your effort?

4. Are you embracing the emotional maturity needed to follow up effectively, or avoiding it out of fear of what you might discover?

5. How are you using technology and AI to track progress, provide support, and keep momentum—without sacrificing the human element?

6. How do you balance follow-up as both a leadership tool and a relationship builder?

Mirror Moment Template: Follow-Up in Action

Date: _____Leadership Situation or Context:

1. Where did I follow up today—and how did it impact the outcome?

1. Was it effective, missed, or delayed?

2. How did my follow-up shape the energy or results?

2. Did I follow up in a way that empowered others—or added pressure?

1. How did the other person respond emotionally or behaviorally?

3. What did my follow-up reveal?

1. Was there a challenge I needed to step into?

2. Did I avoid deeper involvement out of fear or overwhelm?

4. How did I balance accountability with autonomy?

1. Did I offer space for ownership while still guiding the outcome?

5. Am I using tools or systems to support consistent follow-up?

1. What worked well today?

2. Where can I improve—especially with AI or tech?

6. How did my tone, timing, or presence affect the follow-up?

1. Was my communication clear, supportive, and consistent?

7. What follow-up opportunities did I miss—and how will I course correct?

8. Affirmation:

Example: "I lead with consistency and care. My follow-up builds trust, drives action, and reflects my leadership integrity."

Chapter 7

The Key of Recruiting with the End in Mind

"**B**egin with the end in mind to build a team that aligns with your vision." – Stephen Covey

Recruiting doesn't just fill seats—it shapes culture, direction and long-term success. The Key of Recruiting with the End in Mind is rooted in clarity: clarity about your values, your culture, your goals, and the kind of people you want to build those goals with.

A great hire can elevate a team, strengthen culture, and accelerate success. The wrong hire, however, can disrupt momentum, drain morale, and cost far more than just time and money. Recruiting with the end in mind ensures you hire not just for today—but for where you're going tomorrow.

Understanding the Bigger Picture

Effective recruiting begins with a clear understanding of your vision and culture.

While overseeing the launch of multiple retail and restaurant concepts in the United States and Latin America, I quickly realized that technical qualifications alone weren't enough. Many candidates looked great on paper—but lacked the values, adaptability, and team mindset needed to succeed in a fast-paced, mission-driven environment.

That experience taught me that recruiting is strategic—not transactional. When we started hiring based on character, alignment, and long-term potential—not just resumes—we built stronger teams and developed more sustainable operations.

Aligning Recruitment with Organizational Goals

Recruiting with the end in mind means hiring based on where you're going, not just where you are.

In a large-scale international expansion I led in the casual dining space, we worked closely with regional leaders to define what success looked like—not just for individual roles, but for the organization as a whole. We created custom hiring profiles that factored in local market needs, brand expectations, and long-term culture fit.

By aligning hiring practices with organizational goals, we created consistency across regions and dramatically reduced turnover. The people we hired didn't just fit the job—they fit the mission.

Developing a Strategic Recruitment Process

A strategic recruitment process is the blueprint for building a high-performing team. It's not just about filling a vacancy—it's about attracting individuals who will thrive in your culture, contribute meaningfully to your mission, and grow with your organization over time.

Here are the foundational pillars to building a recruitment process that aligns with long-term success:

1. Define Core Values and Skills

2. Craft a Purpose-Driven Job Description

3. Use Structured Interviewing

4. Assess Cultural Alignment

5. Involve the Right People in the Process

6. Pre-Boarding and Expectations Setting

A strategic recruitment process filters for potential, screens for alignment, and sets the stage for long-term growth—not just a quick hire.

Using Technology Without Losing Human Leadership

Technology has revolutionized the recruitment process—but it must be used strategically, not just efficiently. Use platforms and tools that:

1. Track applicants

2. Support structured interviewing

3. Provide hiring analytics

4. Strengthen communication and connection

Artificial Intelligence (AI) has added even more potential to the process. Today, AI tools can:

1. Screen resumes for specific skills and experience

2. Assess personality or communication styles through predictive algorithms

3. Automate outreach and scheduling

4. Flag potential red flags or mismatches

Used wisely, AI can help eliminate bias, save time, and surface candidates who may otherwise get lost in the shuffle. But there's a critical warning here: don't outsource your intuition. Technology should support human judgment—not replace it. Great hiring still comes down to your ability to listen deeply, observe attentively, and discern alignment with your vision.

Technology helps you scale. But leadership helps you choose.

Overcoming Recruitment Challenges

Recruiting isn't without its hurdles. Challenges like high turnover, talent shortages, unconscious bias, disengaged candidates, and mismatched expectations require strategy—not just reaction.

But there's another challenge few leaders talk about: the emotional and cultural cost of the wrong hire. A bad hire doesn't just underperform—they can erode trust, lower morale, and create conflict that ripples throughout the team. When someone joins a team who doesn't align with your culture or vision, your strongest players may start questioning the direction—and even their place—within the organization.

I've seen firsthand how one mismatched hire can derail momentum, create unnecessary drama, and exhaust team leaders. And when leaders don't address it quickly or effectively, it undermines their credibility. This is why recruiting must be approached as a core leadership responsibility, not just an operational task. Every hire sends a message to your team about what you value, what you tolerate, and where you're headed.

Key leadership solutions include:

1. Creating internal pipelines

2. Partnering with schools and training institutions

3. Standardizing interview practices

4. Setting clear, realistic expectations

5. Building relationships throughout the process

6. Embracing the responsibility to guard the culture, not just fill roles

The strongest recruitment systems grow stronger by learning from these challenges—and growing through them as leaders.

Recruiting Through Crisis and Growth Phases

Most organizations recruit when they're comfortable—when things are stable and predictable. But real leadership is tested when recruiting during times of uncertainty or explosive growth.

During periods of crisis, recruiting often feels like an afterthought. Resources are tight, priorities shift, and leaders may fall into survival mode. But this is exactly when recruiting with the end in mind becomes most essential. When I led operations through economic downturns and public health crises, the instinct might have been to freeze hiring or make quick fixes. But we did the opposite—we doubled down on clarity. We asked: What kind of team will help us rebuild stronger on the other side of this? And we hired accordingly.

That mindset kept us anchored in vision while others scrambled. We didn't just hire for recovery—we hired for resilience.

On the other side of the spectrum, growth phases present their own risks. When you're scaling fast, it's easy to prioritize speed over alignment. But growing without intentional recruiting is like building a skyscraper without measuring your foundation. The cracks will show later—in turnover, dysfunction, or cultural drift.

Whether you're hiring in a downturn or an upturn, recruiting with the end in mind ensures your decisions serve the future, not just the moment. It's not about how quickly you fill a role—it's about how intentionally you choose who joins your mission.

Building a Talent Pipeline

You don't build a winning team by reacting—you build it by preparing.

The best leaders and organizations never scramble when a position opens up. Why? Because they've invested in a talent pipeline—a proactive network of people who are ready (or almost ready) to step into key roles.

A talent pipeline includes more than just former applicants or team members. It includes future leaders you've helped shape before they ever applied.

One of the most effective ways to build that kind of pipeline is by teaming up with schools and institutions that train individuals in your industry. Whether it's culinary academies, business schools, hospitality programs, or trade schools, these institutions are filled with people who are learning the technical side—but still need exposure to the real-world side of the industry.

During my leadership journey, I've had the opportunity to partner with several schools that train students in hospitality, business management, and culinary arts. We offered internship programs that gave students their first real experience working with a high-performance team. Not only did they gain real skills—they also got to experience the culture, pace, and standards of a professional environment.

And here's the powerful part: many of those interns went on to become full-time team members. They were already trained, already aligned with our expectations, and already connected to the mission. It was a win for them—and a win for us.

Steps to Build a Sustainable Talent Pipeline:

1. Partner with Schools and Training InstitutionsReach out to schools in your field to offer internships, mentorships, or part-time opportunities.

2. Offer Internship Programs with IntentionDon't just give interns busy work—give them real responsibility, coaching, and exposure to your culture.

3. Stay Connected with Alumni and Former Team Members-Build long-term relationships with people who've worked with you—they may return stronger.

4. Engage with the CommunitySpeak at schools, attend job fairs, and make your presence felt where future leaders are forming.

5. Create a Database of Future TalentTrack standout interns, former employees, and potential hires. Stay in touch. Be ready.

A strong pipeline gives you more than access to talent—it gives you time to develop it. You stop reacting to vacancies and start building a legacy of leadership, one relationship at a time.

The Importance of Onboarding

Hiring someone is only the beginning—their real journey starts on Day One. A strong onboarding program is about culture, connection, and clarity.

It creates belonging, builds confidence, and prevents early turnover. It also teaches new team members how to lead themselves by aligning them with your expectations, your values, and your vision.

Keys to a great onboarding experience:

1. Make it personal

2. Train for culture, not just tasks

3. Establish early mentorship

4. Set up regular check-ins

5. Celebrate their arrival

A great onboarding process doesn't just teach people what to do—it shows them who they can become.

Measuring Recruitment Success

Recruiting doesn't end when a hire is made. It ends when the hire succeeds.

Track metrics like:

    1. Time-to-hire

    2. Quality-of-hire

    3. Retention rates

    4. Candidate experience scores

Use the data to refine your strategy and improve every stage of the hiring journey.

Conclusion

The Key of Recruiting with the End in Mind is about looking beyond the resume. It's about building a team that will grow with you, reflect your values, and push your vision forward.

As a leader, every hire you make either brings your culture closer to what you want—or further from it. When you recruit with purpose, intention, and alignment, you build something far more powerful than just a workforce. You build a legacy.

And as recruitment continues to evolve, so must our tools. Artificial Intelligence (AI) is becoming an increasingly valuable asset in the recruitment process. From resume screening and skills-matching to candidate outreach and communication, AI tools are helping leaders recruit faster and smarter.

Used correctly, AI can improve efficiency, reduce bias, and expand access to high-potential candidates. But it's still just a tool. The heart of recruiting is—and always will be—your ability to spot character, lead with values, and invest in people who reflect your mission.

Key Takeaways

1. Hire with the destination in mind. Align every hire with your values, culture, and long-term vision—not just to fill a role, but to shape the future.

2. Recruiting is leadership. Every hiring decision reflects your maturity, values, and commitment to the culture you're building.

3. Process matters. A structured, intentional recruitment system prevents costly mistakes, strengthens team alignment, and builds long-term success.

4. Culture over credentials. Skills can be taught. Character, adaptability, and team fit are non-negotiable.

5. Build before you need. Internships, school partnerships, and alumni relationships help you develop and invest in future talent before urgency hits.

6. Onboarding is where leadership meets loyalty. Day One is your opportunity to inspire connection, confidence, and purpose.

7. Technology—including AI—can enhance your recruitment process, but human discernment, empathy, and values must always lead the way.

8. Crisis or growth, recruiting with intention keeps your vision intact while others scramble to keep up.

Reflective Questions

1. How clearly have you defined the values, traits, and mindset you want your future team to embody?

2. In what ways has your past hiring helped—or hurt—your team's morale, culture, or long-term direction?

3. Are you proactively building a strong talent pipeline, or reacting when it's too late?

4. How do you handle recruitment during times of crisis or rapid growth—and what might need to shift in your strategy?

5. What does your onboarding process currently communicate about your leadership and expectations?

6. Are you using AI and other technologies to amplify your leadership—or to replace parts of it that require human connection?

7. What is one bold action you can take this quarter to recruit with the end in mind?

Mirror Moment Template: Recruiting with the End in Mind

Date: _____ Position or Hiring Situation: _____

1. What role or position am I currently hiring (or preparing to hire) for?

    1. Am I hiring for where we are—or where we're going?

2. How clearly have I defined the values, skills, and cultural traits needed for this role?

3. Is my current recruitment process structured and strategic—or reactive and rushed?

    1. What needs to be added or improved?

4. Am I assessing alignment with our mission and culture—or just resumes and qualifications?

5. What lessons have I learned from past hiring mistakes—and how will I apply them now?

6. Am I leveraging technology and AI wisely—without outsourcing my intuition?

7. How am I recruiting during this season (growth, stability, or crisis)?

   1. What shifts in mindset or strategy are required?

8. What am I doing to build a talent pipeline for the future—not just solve today's problems?

9. Affirmation:

Example: "I hire with vision, build with purpose, and lead with people who reflect our mission."

Chapter 8

The Key of Trust

"Trust is the glue of life. It's the most essential ingredient in effective communication and the foundation of all relationships." – **Stephen Covey**

Trust is the foundation of every strong team. Without it, even the most talented group will fail to achieve its potential. The Key of Trust involves building relationships based on honesty, reliability, transparency, and respect. It's not something you demand—it's something you earn, one action, one conversation, one decision at a time.

The Importance of Trust in Leadership

Trust isn't just a leadership principle—it's the foundation that every other leadership principle stands on. Without trust, no system, strategy, or structure will hold up over time. Trust is the invisible contract between a leader and their team, and when it's strong, it fuels performance, loyalty, creativity, and resilience.

In leadership, your influence is only as strong as the trust others place in you. You can have authority from a title, but without trust, your ability to lead effectively is limited. A leader may get compliance through fear or control—but only trust creates commitment. And commitment is what fuels people to go above and beyond, to stay engaged through adversity, and to believe in the mission you're driving.

During my tenure at a large food and beverage group, I inherited a team that was skeptical and demoralized. Leadership changes had left them uncertain, and morale was at an all-time low. The turnover rate was high, the culture was fractured, and no one was speaking openly. The issue wasn't talent—it was trust. No initiative would work, no system would stick, until that gap was closed.

So I didn't start with numbers or performance metrics. I started with transparency and presence. I scheduled a team meeting and said the words they needed to hear most: "I understand where you've been, and I'm here to rebuild what's been broken." That one act of vulnerability shifted the energy in the room. From there, I backed it up with consistent communication, follow-through, and one-on-one conversations.

Trust unlocks engagement. It gives people the safety to speak up, to take risks, and to make decisions. Teams that trust their leader don't waste energy second-guessing motives or protecting themselves—they focus on outcomes, innovation, and shared success.

Trust also protects your team during hard times. Whether you're dealing with layoffs, restructuring, a crisis, or even just growing pains, people will stick with you if they believe you're being honest and that you care about their future—not just your own.

Leadership without trust is like trying to drive a high-performance vehicle with no fuel. You can have the best vision, the best systems, the best strategies—but if people don't believe in you, none of it will matter. On the other hand, leadership built on trust can take an ordinary team and achieve extraordinary things.

Trust is what transforms a group into a mission-driven unit. It's what allows feedback to become growth instead of defensiveness. It's what empowers individuals to lead themselves. And most importantly—it's what turns you from a manager into a leader worth following.

Building Trust Through Transparency

Transparency is the foundation of trust—and one of the most powerful tools in a leader's hands. It doesn't mean telling people everything; it means not hiding anything that affects them. It means sharing the "why" behind decisions, owning mistakes, communicating frequently, and creating a culture where clarity wins over confusion.

People don't expect leaders to have all the answers—but they do expect honesty. They expect to be included in the journey, especially when their roles and futures are directly impacted. When a leader is open, honest, and vulnerable, it signals respect. It tells your team: "You matter. You deserve the truth."

I've seen time and time again that a lack of information breeds fear, doubt, and assumptions. When people don't know what's happening or why, they begin filling in the blanks—and usually not in your favor. But when you lead with transparency, you replace speculation with security. You show that you trust them enough to share the truth.

In one leadership role, I launched weekly "State of the Business" huddles where I shared key wins, challenges, and upcoming changes. I broke down performance metrics in ways that made sense to every team member—whether they were in management, operations, or part-time support. I also made space for feedback and suggestions in real time.

What happened next was powerful: team members started thinking like owners. Because they had visibility into the business, they began suggesting ways to cut waste, increase efficiency, and improve customer experience. Transparency turned disengaged workers into partners. They weren't just doing their jobs anymore—they were helping drive the mission.

Here's how transparency builds trust in practical terms:

1. It reduces fear – When people know what's going on, they stop wasting energy on "what ifs."

2. It increases accountability – When you share openly, people feel a deeper responsibility to uphold their role in the bigger picture.

3. It strengthens loyalty – Teams don't follow perfect leaders—they follow real ones.

4. It invites collaboration – When people feel included, they offer ideas instead of complaints.

Ways to Build Transparency into Your Leadership Style:

1. Communicate Early and Often

2. Share the Why, Not Just the What

3. Address the Difficult Topics

4. Own Your Mistakes Publicly

5. Show Them the Numbers (When Appropriate)

Transparency isn't weakness—it's leadership maturity. It requires courage to lead with openness, especially when the news is tough or uncertain. But in those moments, people learn who you really are—and that's when trust becomes unshakable.

The Role of Consistency in Trust

Trust isn't built in bold gestures—it's built in the quiet, everyday moments where consistency matters most. A leader who keeps their word, delivers on promises, and remains level-headed under pressure becomes a reliable anchor in uncertain times.

In a previous leadership role, I made it a point to follow through on even the small things: a scheduled one-on-one, a promised resource, a commitment to review a process. Those seemingly minor actions built something major—trust. And when people trust you, they'll follow you through uncertainty with confidence.

Overcoming Barriers to Trust

Rebuilding trust is one of the hardest—but most rewarding—things a leader can do. Whether the damage was caused by a previous leader, a toxic culture, or an isolated event, restoring trust takes more than good intentions. It requires action, humility, and time.

I once stepped into a leadership role where the department had completely lost confidence in leadership. Rumors replaced facts, silence replaced feedback, and walls replaced collaboration.

I started where any true leader must—by listening. I didn't assume I knew what needed to be fixed. I asked. I created space for my team to voice frustrations without fear of judgment. Yes, I held one-on-ones—and I'll say this with emphasis: one-on-ones, done consistently and with care, are not just check-ins—they are trust-building appointments.

From there, I took what I learned and turned it into visible action. I didn't try to fix everything overnight. Instead, I focused on small wins. I built momentum. I backed my words with follow-through. That team didn't turn around because of one speech or a new policy—they transformed because they saw I was willing to earn their trust, not demand it.

In rebuilding trust, your goal isn't perfection—it's consistency. Teams don't expect leaders to be flawless; they want leaders who show up, follow through, and lead with integrity.

Common Barriers to Rebuilding Trust and How to Overcome Them:

1. Politics and Backstabbing – Gossip, hidden agendas, and backchanneling destroy trust faster than almost anything else. When team members believe others are working against them—or that their reputation is under attack behind closed doors—they become defensive, disengaged, or even combative. To fix this, leaders must address issues directly and model transparency. Establish a zero-tolerance policy for gossip and passive-aggressive behavior. Promote open dialogue where concerns are brought forward respectfully and resolved in real time. Create a culture where problems are addressed with people—not about them.

2. Past Leadership Trauma – Acknowledge it. Don't pretend it didn't happen.

3. Lack of Follow-Through – Even small broken promises weaken trust.

4. Poor Communication – Confusion erodes confidence.

5. Fear of Retaliation – People must feel safe to be honest.

6. Emotional Inconsistency – Stability in behavior creates safety.

Steps to Rebuild Trust:
1. Address Toxic Behavior Directly, Start by calling out backbiting, gossip, and passive-aggressive behavior the moment it surfaces. Don't ignore it or pretend it's harmless—these actions silently destroy trust. Instead, create an environment where direct and respectful communication is the norm, and model it in every interaction.

2. Acknowledge Past Mistakes

3. Engage in Active Listening

4. Implement Visible Changes

5. Be Patient

6. Stay Present

Trust and Decision-Making

Trust makes hard decisions easier to carry. When a team believes in your intent, they don't need to agree with every decision to support it.

I once had to reduce team hours during a seasonal slowdown. I explained the reasoning, how long it would last, and what we were doing to support affected team members. Because we had trust, the team leaned in—not away. They didn't panic. They adapted. That's the power of trust.

Trust as a Two-Way Street

It's not just about your team trusting you—you must trust them too. Delegation is an act of trust. Empowering someone to lead a project, make a decision, or represent the brand communicates something powerful: "I believe in you."

In a leadership role expanding operations in Latin America, I gave regional managers full autonomy to adapt the brand to their markets. The results? Faster execution, stronger engagement, and local innovation I couldn't have created on my own.

Trust multiplies when it flows both ways.

Practical Strategies for Building Trust

1. Lead by Example

2. Foster Open Communication

3. Provide Consistent Feedback

4. Invest in Relationships

5. Protect the Culture

Trust and Team Dynamics

Trust isn't a buzzword—it's what transforms a group into a team. At one concept I helped launch, we used team-building sessions to break down barriers. These weren't just games—they were conversations, problem-solving challenges, and exercises where people saw each other as humans, not just roles.

The difference was real. Conflict became collaboration. Silence became feedback. Teams stopped competing—and started building together.

Measuring Trust Within Your Team

Trust isn't always easy to see, but it leaves clues. Some ways to measure it include:

    1. Anonymous Feedback Surveys

    2. Engagement and Turnover Metrics

    3. Team Participation and Conflict Resolution

    4. Peer Recognition

Trust and Feedback Culture

One of the most powerful signs of trust is the ability to give and receive feedback—honestly, constructively, and consistently. Without trust, feedback is either avoided or becomes a weapon. But with trust, feedback becomes a mirror for growth.

In my experience, the strongest teams are not the ones with the fewest conflicts—they are the ones who know how to talk through those conflicts. They've created a culture where it's okay to challenge ideas without challenging the person. That's only possible in an environment rooted in trust.

One thing I've always encouraged is upward feedback—giving your team permission (and even an invitation) to give feedback to you as a leader. It communicates humility and reinforces the belief that everyone's voice matters.

To build a feedback culture grounded in trust:

1. Normalize feedback in everyday interactions

2. Model it yourself by asking for feedback regularly

3. Train your team on how to give feedback that is respectful, timely, and specific

4. Reward vulnerability and honesty, even when it's uncomfortable

Feedback is not about being right—it's about getting better. And trust is what makes that journey possible.

The Long-Term Benefits of Trust

Trust isn't just a "soft skill"—it's a hard advantage. Teams built on trust innovate faster, recover quicker, and outperform others in both good and difficult times.

I've seen firsthand how trust fuels loyalty, creativity, and resilience. It reduces politics, increases ownership, and creates a culture where people do more than they're asked—because they believe in what they're building.

Conclusion

The Key of Trust is not just foundational—it's transformational. It's the difference between a team that functions and a team that flourishes. Between a leader who gets results and one who creates lasting impact.

Trust cannot be rushed or faked. It's earned moment by moment, through the way you speak, the way you listen, and the way you follow through when no one's watching. It's revealed not only when things are going well, but especially when they're not—when there's pressure, tension, or uncertainty. That's when your team learns who you really are. And that's when your leadership either builds or breaks trust.

Through transparency, you make people feel seen. Through consistency, you make people feel safe. Through emotional steadiness, you create a culture where people are free to be honest, make mistakes, and grow. And through accountability—starting with yourself—you show that trust is not just expected, but modeled.

When trust is strong, teams move faster, innovate more boldly, and recover more quickly. Conflict becomes collaboration. Feedback becomes growth. Responsibility becomes ownership. And leadership becomes influence—not by force, but by earned respect.

And here's what's most powerful: trust multiplies. When your team sees you trusting them—giving them autonomy, listening with presence, empowering them to lead—it invites them to rise. It transforms your role from boss to coach, from manager to mentor, from director to developer of people.

If your leadership journey is a marathon, then trust is the road you're running on. Everything else—vision, strategy, systems, execution—depends on its strength.

So invest in it. Nurture it. Protect it. Rebuild it when needed. Because the leader who builds trust doesn't just create success—they create something far more rare: a team that believes, belongs, and becomes better together. Trust also has a measurable impact on performance—it increases efficiency, customer satisfaction, and ultimately, revenue. When trust is high, teams are more collaborative, accountable, and proactive, which directly contributes to business growth and profitability. On the flip side, a lack of trust creates friction, miscommunication, and disengagement—leading to missed targets, lost customers, and financial setbacks. If trust is the fuel of high performance, then a deficit of it is the silent drain that bleeds momentum and results.

Key Takeaways

1. Trust is the foundation of leadership. Without it, your title is just a word—trust is what turns it into real influence.

2. Transparency builds connection. When you openly share the "why" behind decisions, people feel seen, valued, and included.

3. Consistency creates safety. When your behavior and words are steady, your team can focus on performance—not managing your unpredictability.

4. Trust must be rebuilt before it can be regained. Acknowledge the past, listen with humility, and turn feedback into visible change.

5. Trust is not a one-way street. As a leader, you must also show trust—through delegation, empowerment, and belief in your people's potential.

6. Trust transforms conflict into collaboration. Teams that trust each other can handle tension, challenge ideas, and grow stronger through it.

7. Small actions matter. Keeping your word, showing up on time, and giving honest feedback are the bricks that build the house of trust.

8. One-on-ones are a trust-building tool. Used consistently, they show presence, care, and commitment to individual growth.

9. Trust multiplies. When your team feels trusted, they rise to the occasion—and they begin to trust each other, too.

10. Emotional steadiness is a signal of leadership maturity. Trust isn't just about what you do—it's about how you carry yourself, especially under pressure.

11. Trust adds to revenue and profits. A high-trust environment drives better collaboration, innovation, and ownership—which leads to stronger business performance. Conversely, a lack of trust causes disengagement, inefficiency, and financial setbacks.

Reflective Questions

1. What consistent actions in your daily leadership either build or break trust? How can you reinforce the former and eliminate the latter?

2. Have you ever avoided addressing political behavior like gossip or backstabbing? How might that be affecting your team's trust?

3. Where in your organization has trust been damaged, and

what concrete steps can you take to restore it?

4. How transparent are you with your team when it comes to decisions that impact them—especially during uncertain or difficult times?

5. In what ways do you demonstrate trust in others through delegation, feedback, and empowerment?

6. How are you building a culture where feedback—both giving and receiving—is seen as a tool for growth rather than criticism?

7. Are your one-on-one meetings being used to strengthen relationships and accountability—or are they just task check-ins?

8. What measurable impact (positive or negative) has trust had on your team's performance, collaboration, and revenue outcomes?

9. Do your team members feel emotionally safe in your presence? What could you do to increase that sense of psychological safety?

10. What systems or habits can you implement this month to reinforce trust as a daily leadership practice?

Mirror Moment Template: Trust

Date: _____Team/Organization: _____

1. Where is trust currently strong within your team—and where is it weakest?

2. What's one consistent behavior you model that builds trust—and one that might unintentionally erode it?

3. Have you avoided addressing politics, gossip, or back-channeling in your team? Why?

4. What is one vulnerable truth you need to share with your team that would build greater transparency and credibility?

5. Do your current systems (1-on-1s, meetings, check-ins) foster trust—or just track tasks?

6. When was the last time you received feedback from your team? What did you learn—and how did you respond?

7. What measurable results (sales, morale, retention, etc.) might be impacted by the current level of trust in your leadership?

8. Affirmation:

Example: "I lead with honesty, follow through with integrity, and create a culture where trust is not just expected—it is experienced."

Chapter 9

The Key of Living from Solutions

"**S**tay focused on the solution, not the problem, and watch possibilities unfold." – Tony Robbins

Every leader will face problems. What separates average leaders from great ones is how they respond. The Key of Living from Solutions is not about avoiding problems—it's about refusing to live in them. It's about shifting your mindset from complaint to creativity, from reaction to responsibility.

This key unlocks forward momentum, emotional discipline, and sustainable progress. Leaders who live from solutions inspire innovation, reduce internal friction, and equip their teams to thrive through uncertainty.

Problems are inevitable. But staying stuck in them? That's a choice.

Embracing a Solutions-Oriented Mindset

Early in my leadership journey, I didn't always lead with this mindset. When something went wrong, I'd get caught in the frustration, replaying what had happened, blaming circumstances or people. I learned the hard way that while reflection has value, rumination does not.

One pivotal moment came during my time overseeing operations for a hospitality company. A critical vendor failure disrupted our supply chain, throwing schedules and customer satisfaction into chaos. My initial reaction was frustration. But the longer I stayed in that mode, the more time I was wasting. I made a conscious decision to shift. I gathered the team, clarified what was within our control, identified alternate suppliers, and created new protocols for contingency planning.

That experience showed me something that stuck: solutions create momentum. Problems paralyze. Leadership demands that we choose progress.

Training Your Team to Think in Solutions

A solutions-oriented culture doesn't happen by accident. It must be intentionally modeled, taught, and reinforced—starting with leadership, then filtering down through every level of the organization. The best leaders don't just solve problems; they develop people who can solve problems without them.

In one of my leadership roles within the hospitality and retail industries, I inherited a team that had been conditioned to only point out what was wrong—never what could be done about it. Every meeting was a list of complaints, every challenge met with a chorus of "This won't work." But I knew that if I wanted a culture of ownership, I had to train my team not just to recognize problems—but to bring solutions with them.

I introduced a simple but powerful rule: "If you bring a problem to the table, you must also bring at least one potential solution." This rule changed our conversations overnight. Team members began shifting from blame to brainstorming. It taught them to think like owners, not employees.

Here are several ways to train your team to think in solutions:

1. Model It Relentlessly

2. Create a Safe Environment for Ideas

3. Use the "3 Before Me" Rule

4. Coach the Process, Not Just the Outcome

5. Host Solution Labs or Innovation Hours

By consistently encouraging and rewarding solution-focused thinking, your team begins to adopt the belief: "Problems don't define us—how we respond to them does."

Solutions-Focused Communication

Clear, forward-focused communication is the engine that powers a solutions-oriented culture. It's not just what you say—it's how you say it, and what mindset you create when you say it. Great leaders know that language shapes reality. If your communication always centers on what went wrong, your team will stay anchored in the past. But if you shift the conversation toward what can be done next, you unlock energy, creativity, and momentum.

Here are key ways to practice solutions-focused communication:

1. Reframe the Narrative

2. Use the Language of Possibility

3. Debrief Constructively

4. Lead with Emotional Steadiness

5. Encourage Upward Feedback

The benefits? You reduce blame, increase clarity, speed up execution, and energize your culture. Communication done right becomes a forward-moving force that keeps teams aligned, engaged, and empowered.

The Role of Resilience in Solution-Finding

Resilience is the backbone of a solutions-oriented mindset. It's what enables leaders to stay calm, respond with clarity, and keep moving forward when challenges pile up. During the COVID-19 pandemic, operational shutdowns threatened the survival of businesses across multiple industries. I worked with a leadership team to pivot quickly—launching delivery services, creating digital campaigns, and retraining staff. These actions didn't just preserve jobs—they paved the way for long-term growth.

But resilience goes beyond crisis management. It's a daily discipline. It's the habit of showing up grounded, emotionally balanced, and ready to lead from strength. Resilient leaders don't avoid stress—they transform it. They bounce forward, not just back. And they give their teams the courage to do the same.

Resilience also means allowing room for emotional honesty without becoming paralyzed by it. It's okay to acknowledge disappointment or fatigue—but then ask: "What's still possible?"

You build resilience by:

1. Practicing mindfulness and emotional regulation

2. Creating space for recovery and rest

3. Focusing on what's in your control

4. Framing failure as feedback, not finality

The more resilient you are as a leader, the more your team mirrors that energy. In fast-moving industries or high-stress seasons, resilience becomes your greatest competitive advantage.

Creating Systems to Support Solutions

In one company I led, we introduced a "Solution Log"—a shared document where employees logged issues, actions taken, and outcomes. It became a running record of lessons learned and empowered every department to build on each other's insights.

But that was just one piece of the puzzle. Creating a system to support solutions means designing your operations, communication, and team rhythms in ways that promote clarity, agility, and accountability. You don't want your team improvising how to respond to every challenge—you want to give them a clear process that supports consistent, creative responses.

We also developed:

1. **Team scoreboards** that tracked progress against goals, with visual cues for performance trends.

2. **Weekly solution standups**, where each department shared one challenge and one proposed fix—encouraging cross-pollination of ideas.

3. **Digital feedback loops**, where anonymous suggestions could be submitted, reviewed, and responded to in a timely, transparent way.

Strong systems do more than organize workflow—they shape behavior. They help people think proactively, share knowledge, and stay accountable without being micromanaged. And when those systems are reinforced by leadership behavior and cultural values, they become more than tools—they become part of how the organization thinks.

Key Elements of Supportive Systems:

1. **Clarity** – Everyone understands the process, expectations, and purpose behind each system.

2. **Accessibility** – Tools and documents are easy to find, use, and contribute to.

3. **Feedback Loops** – Every action produces learning. Systems should evolve based on what's working.

When you create systems that support solution-thinking, you're not just managing today's problems—you're training your team to solve tomorrow's.

Avoiding Pitfalls in a Solutions-Oriented Approach

Leading from solutions is powerful—but it's not without its traps. If you're not careful, you can unintentionally create a culture that values speed over strategy, fixes over foundations, or positivity over honesty. Being solutions-focused doesn't mean ignoring reality—it means responding to it with clarity and intention.

Here are some common pitfalls leaders face when driving a solutions-oriented culture—and how to avoid them:

1. Addressing Symptoms Instead of Root Causes

2. Rushing Decisions Under Pressure

3. Silencing Valuable Feedback in the Name of Positivity

4. Over-Relying on the Same Problem-Solvers

5. Confusing Busyness with Progress

When you avoid these common pitfalls, you don't just create a solutions-driven culture—you build a wise, resilient, and empowered team that solves the right problems the right way.

Success Stories of Living from Solutions

In the retail and food sector, particularly in New York City, I've led turnarounds in underperforming locations that many had written off as lost causes. These units were plagued by poor service, high employee turnover, and consistent financial losses. At first glance, it seemed like a staffing or sales problem. But when I took a deeper look, the real issue wasn't a lack of talent—it was a lack of systems and a mindset that defaulted to blame instead of action.

I implemented team-wide workshops on ownership, introduced daily leadership huddles focused on proactive thinking, and created scoreboards that celebrated progress over perfection. We didn't waste time pointing fingers. We spent our energy identifying quick wins, eliminating inefficiencies, and listening to frontline input.

Within six months, that location saw a 25% increase in revenue—but that was just the beginning. In a year and a half, that once-underperforming store became the number one location in the entire company in nearly every major metric:

1. Revenue

2. Profits

3. Customer Satisfaction

4. Employee Retention

5. Sales per Manhour

6. Cost Control

And just as importantly—the emotional transformation was undeniable. The very same employees who had once been disengaged and demotivated were now proud, energized, and honored to be part of something great. They wore their location's success like a badge of honor—because they didn't just witness the turnaround; they were the reason it happened.

And this wasn't a small startup—we're talking about one of the largest brands in its industry in the United States at the time. That transformation didn't happen because we brought in some outside savior—it happened because we built a solutions-first culture from the inside out.

In another project while expanding operations across Latin America, logistical and supply issues emerged just weeks before a major launch. The easy reaction would have been to delay and blame external vendors. But instead, we created a rapid-response team composed of local managers, regional suppliers, and logistics partners. That team worked around the clock for five days—collaborating in real time and testing temporary solutions until permanent ones could be implemented. Not only did we meet the opening deadline, but the experience created deep trust and unity across the international leadership team.

Whether it's an urban franchise in Manhattan or a beachside café in Panama, the principle holds true: when you live from solutions, you lead your people out of the problem—and into possibility.

The Ripple Effect of Solutions-Oriented Leadership

The true power of living from solutions isn't just in solving problems—it's in what it creates around you. When a leader chooses to lead with a solutions mindset, it becomes contagious. It inspires teams to stop reacting and start creating. It shifts energy from stress to strategy.

And it lays the foundation for a resilient, high-performance culture that can thrive no matter what challenges come.

In organizations where I've implemented a solutions-first philosophy, the ripple effects have been transformative. Teams that once hesitated to act out of fear of failure started proposing bold ideas. People who were once quiet in meetings found their voice because they knew they were expected to bring ideas, not just observe problems. Leaders at all levels began coaching their teams differently—moving from control to collaboration, from blame to ownership.

Here's what those ripples look like in action:

1. Increased innovation

2. Higher morale

3. Stronger collaboration

4. More efficient execution

5. Stronger emotional intelligence

6. Improved customer experience

7. Leadership bench strength grows

I once had a team member say, "When I started here, I just showed up to do my shift. Now, I come in thinking about how we can improve the experience—for the guest, for my team, and for myself." That's what a solutions culture does—it creates buy-in that goes far beyond metrics. It creates ownership.

The ripple effect of solutions-oriented leadership doesn't end at the walls of your business. It reaches families. It reaches communities. When people learn to stop complaining and start creating solutions, it changes how they parent, how they handle adversity, how they show up in relationships—and ultimately, how they see themselves.

This mindset isn't just good for business. It's good for people. And when leaders commit to building a solutions-first culture, the result is more than profit—it's purpose, progress, and people who are proud of who they are and what they're building together.

Leading Through Crisis with Solutions

Leading through crisis is where your leadership mindset gets tested the most. Crisis doesn't ask for permission—it arrives suddenly, shifts priorities overnight, and often exposes the cracks in your systems and leadership culture.

But crisis also creates clarity. It reveals the strength of your values, the depth of your preparation, and your team's ability to stay solution-focused when pressure is high.

One example came during an unexpected political disruption in one of the countries where our restaurant brand was expanding. The supply chain was interrupted, customer traffic was unstable, and team morale plummeted. Rather than retreat or react emotionally, we activated our solutions mindset. We reassessed our entire weekly operations model, streamlined our vendor strategy, and launched short-term incentives that stabilized customer volume.

The results didn't just help us survive—we earned the trust and loyalty of our local team. That experience didn't break our culture. It deepened it.

Key principles for leading through crisis with solutions:

1. **Act with urgency, not panic.** Move quickly but stay calm. Emotions are contagious—so is clarity.

2. **Use crisis as a teaching opportunity.** Reflect with your team on what worked, what didn't, and what systems need

improvement.

3. **Prioritize communication.** In uncertain times, overcommunication is leadership.

4. **Anchor in purpose.** Help your team see that the mission still matters—and that adversity can sharpen your commitment, not weaken it.

Crises will come. But when your organization is built on a solutions-first culture, you won't crumble. You'll rise—and lead others through it.

Conclusion

The Key of Living from Solutions transforms obstacles into opportunities. It is a mindset that sees beyond the problem and leads others into possibility. By modeling this mindset, training your team to think proactively, and building systems that reinforce accountability and creativity, you create a culture of progress.

Solutions-focused leadership is not just about fixing what's broken—it's about unlocking what's possible. It's about turning setbacks into strategies, fear into focus, and complaints into creative energy.

When leaders adopt this mindset consistently, teams become more resilient, innovation increases, and ownership grows. What once looked like a wall becomes a doorway. What once felt like failure becomes fuel. What once seemed uncertain becomes a chance to lead boldly.

It's also important to remember that living from solutions is not about ignoring pain or bypassing difficulty. It's about standing in the middle of it all—and choosing to move forward anyway. That's real leadership. That's where growth happens.

And the impact goes far beyond day-to-day operations. When you lead from solutions, you're not just solving problems—you're shaping people. You're helping them see what's possible when they choose power over panic, clarity over chaos, and forward movement over fear.

Ultimately, the choice to live and lead from solutions is the choice to lead with purpose. It's how you unlock the next level of your leadership—and help others unlock theirs.

Key Takeaways

1. **Solutions are a mindset.** Problems are inevitable, but choosing to focus on solutions is what separates strong leaders from reactive ones.

2. **Modeling matters.** When leaders demonstrate calm, creativity, and solution-thinking, teams rise to meet that standard.

3. **Train for ownership.** A solutions-first culture begins by teaching and empowering your team to think proactively.

4. **Communication is critical.** Clear, consistent, and constructive dialogue shifts focus from blame to progress.

5. **Resilience sustains progress.** A leader's emotional steadiness enables better decisions and inspires confidence during crisis.

6. **Systems reinforce culture.** Tools like Solution Logs and feedback loops support consistency and drive momentum.

7. **Avoiding common pitfalls protects morale.** Don't rush solutions or silence feedback. Slow down to align with long-term growth.

8. **Living from solutions transforms teams.** It builds confidence, unlocks innovation, and helps people take pride in their growth.

9. **The ripple effect is real.** When solutions-thinking becomes cultural, it extends beyond business into families, communities, and personal identity.

10. **Leading through crisis demands clarity.** Solutions-first leadership becomes the anchor during uncertainty and pressure.

11. **Solutions impact results.** A solution-oriented team doesn't just feel better—they perform better. Revenue, retention, and morale all rise when problem-solving becomes the norm.

12. **Purpose grows through solutions.** When people learn to solve rather than spiral, they gain a sense of meaning in their work and pride in their contribution.

Reflective Questions

1. How can you shift your own mindset from problem-dwelling to solution-creating, especially during high-pressure situations?

2. What habits or daily rituals can you implement to reinforce a solution-oriented culture within your leadership?

3. How are you modeling solution-driven behavior for your team, especially in moments of uncertainty?

4. Are your team meetings framed in possibility and progress—or rooted in blame and barriers?

5. What systems (like Solution Logs) could help your team turn learning into action?

6. How do you currently support resilience within your team, and what can you improve?

7. Have any of the listed pitfalls shown up in your leadership culture, and what steps can you take to correct them?

8. What are the ripple effects you want to create beyond the workplace—and how can a solutions-first mindset help you achieve them?

9. In what ways can your team benefit from practicing ownership instead of waiting for top-down answers?

10. How prepared are you to lead from solutions the next time a crisis strikes—and what steps can you take now to increase that readiness?

Mirror Moment: Living from Solutions
Reflect. Realign. Respond.

Use this mirror moment to break through frustration and move into focused, forward leadership.

Affirmation: *I am a leader who rises above obstacles. I choose clarity over chaos, creativity over complaint, and solutions over stagnation. Every challenge I face is an opportunity to unlock new strength, serve with greater purpose, and lead others into possibility.*

1. Current Challenge *What problem or situation is currently testing your leadership? Describe it clearly and honestly.*

2. Emotional Response *How are you reacting emotionally? (e.g., frustration, fear, defensiveness, overwhelm)*

3. Shift to Ownership *What part of this can you take responsibility for—mindset, communication, preparation, support?*

4. Generate Solutions *List at least 3 actions, ideas, or responses that move the situation forward.*

5. Engage the Team *Who can you involve in co-creating or owning part of the solution?*

6. Next Right Step *What specific action will you take in the next 24 hours to lead from solutions?*

Chapter 10

The Key of Adding Value

"The true measure of a leader is not in how much they achieve, but in how much they help others grow and succeed." – John C. Maxwell

Adding value is at the heart of impactful leadership. The Key of Adding Value emphasizes consistently seeking ways to uplift your team, customers, and organization. Great leaders don't just manage resources—they enrich them.

Defining Value in leadership goes beyond profitability. It encompasses the ways leaders enhance the skills, morale, and opportunities of their teams. In my leadership journey, I recognized that employees often felt undervalued or overlooked. By implementing targeted training programs, offering career development opportunities, and personally acknowledging individual contributions, I witnessed dramatic shifts in morale, engagement, and productivity.

Adding value is about creating an environment where people feel seen, heard, and essential to the mission. When individuals recognize that they are an integral part of something greater than themselves, they rise to the occasion with energy and purpose.

Adding Value to Your Team

1. Invest in Development: Provide your team with tools and resources to grow professionally and personally. For example, launching hands-on workshops or sponsoring leadership training creates not just better workers, but future leaders. A strong development plan shows people you see their potential, which can ignite greater loyalty and performance.

2. Coach with Intent: Coaching is one of the most powerful ways to add value to your team. It involves more than just telling someone what to do—it's about helping them discover how to think critically, make better decisions, and unlock their potential. Great leaders make time for coaching conversations, offering constructive feedback, posing insightful questions, and helping their team members set meaningful personal and professional goals.

3. Practice Active Appreciation: Recognize achievements frequently—not just during annual reviews. Creating systems of appreciation, such as public recognition, personalized notes, or shoutouts during meetings, reminds people their efforts matter.

4. Encourage Innovation: Foster a culture where new ideas are welcomed and rewarded. Innovation hours, team brainstorms, or open-door idea policies give team members ownership and pride in shaping the future.

Enhancing Customer Experience

Adding value extends to the people your organization serves. Customers don't just want products or services—they want meaningful experiences. Leaders who prioritize personalized service, responsiveness, and relationship-building create loyalty that transcends transactions.

Steps to Enhance Customer Value:

1. Understand Their Needs: Regular surveys or simple conversations can yield powerful insights.

2. Exceed Expectations: Go beyond what's expected—surprise and delight wherever possible.

3. Show Gratitude: Loyalty programs, appreciation messages, and attentive service all reinforce value.

Adding Value to the Organization Leaders who think long-term, focus on building lasting value across departments and systems. But building value isn't just about numbers and processes—it's about people. One of the most powerful ways to create organizational success is to care deeply about the individuals who keep it running every day. When leaders value their people, those people, in turn, value the organization.

Caring means listening, being present, showing empathy, and creating an environment where employees feel supported, safe, and empowered. When your team knows they are genuinely cared for, they show up with greater commitment, resilience, and innovation.

Whether through cost-saving innovations, improving workplace culture, or creating better communication pipelines, strategic decision-making drives sustainable growth. But it's the care we extend to our people that sustains momentum and fosters loyalty through every season of change.

I once helped restructure operations in a company that was profitable but burning out its workforce. By reengineering workflows, cross-training employees, and increasing transparency, we preserved margins while boosting retention and engagement.

Creating a Legacy of Adding value is not just about today's performance—it's about tomorrow's impact. Mentorship, succession planning, and cultural shaping ensure that your influence extends far beyond your immediate circle.

True legacy is not measured in revenue or market share—it's measured in how many lives you've touched, how many leaders you've lifted, and how many people are better because of your presence. To create a legacy of value, you must first lead with intention. Every conversation, every decision, and every challenge is an opportunity to plant seeds of growth in others.

It also means being committed to the development of future leaders. This is more than offering promotions—it's about sharing wisdom, modeling integrity, and offering opportunities to lead, even when it's inconvenient. When you pour into others, you create a ripple effect that can influence generations.

Legacy is also about values. What do you stand for? What will your people say you represented long after you're gone? When your values guide your actions, they become embedded into your organization's culture, ensuring that the standards you uphold today will endure tomorrow.

I've made it a priority throughout my career to mentor rising leaders, sharing the tools and mindset that helped me succeed. Watching those individuals thrive in their own right is one of the most rewarding outcomes of my leadership journey. And the greatest compliment I've ever received is when someone said, "Because of your belief in me, I believed in myself." That is the essence of legacy: helping others rise above what they thought was impossible.

Challenges in Adding Value

1. Balancing Short-Term and Long-Term Goals – Sometimes adding value requires sacrificing immediate wins for sustainable growth. Leaders often face pressure from stakeholders to deliver quick results, but true leadership means maintaining the courage to advocate for investments in people, process, and culture that may take time to bear fruit. The challenge lies in communicating the vision clearly enough that your team understands why today's sacrifice paves the way for tomorrow's success.

2. Overcoming Resistance to Change – Adding value usually involves introducing new ideas, strategies, or expectations—and not everyone is immediately on board. People naturally resist what's unfamiliar, especially if past change efforts have failed or felt top-down. The key is empathy and inclusion. Involve your team in shaping the change. Listen to their concerns. Celebrate small wins along the way. When people feel they are part of the process, they become advocates instead of skeptics.

3. Resource Constraints – Time, money, and manpower are limited, particularly in fast-paced or under-resourced environments. Leaders often wonder how they can give more when there's barely enough to go around. But adding value doesn't always require large investments. Sometimes a five-minute conversation, a handwritten note, or a small gesture of trust can make all the difference. Start small, be consistent, and build momentum.

4. Maintaining Consistency – Adding value isn't a one-time

effort—it's a mindset and a habit. During times of stress, leaders are tempted to revert to command-and-control approaches or skip the small things that show appreciation. But consistency builds culture. It's the ongoing, everyday effort to invest in people that creates deep roots and lasting trust. Systems, rituals, and accountability partners can help keep value-adding behaviors front and center, even when things get hectic.

5. Avoiding Burnout While Giving – Leaders who are committed to pouring into others can sometimes forget to refill their own cup. Over time, this leads to emotional exhaustion, decreased empathy, and resentment. The most effective value-givers are those who know how to step back, reflect, recharge, and grow themselves. Invest in your own leadership development, surround yourself with people who inspire and challenge you, and create boundaries that allow you to sustain the energy required to lead with generosity.

Practical Tools for Adding Value

1. Value Mapping: Identify areas of greatest need and potential impact.

2. Feedback Mechanisms: Regular check-ins, surveys, and conversations offer insight and show respect.

3. Recognition Systems: Praise and rewards—formal and informal—drive passion.

4. Coaching Frameworks: Clear goals, progress tracking, and personal development plans.

5. Development Calendars: Plan learning and mentorship throughout the year.

6. Culture Audits: Evaluate how well your values show up in daily culture.

7. Time and Presence: Sometimes the most valuable gift is your undivided attention.

Success Stories of Adding Value in Sarasota, Florida, I worked with a team struggling with low engagement and high turnover. Employees were disengaged, siloed, and lacked cross-functional understanding. We launched a cross-training program that allowed team members to rotate across different departments. The result wasn't just improved flexibility and productivity—it also brought about a cultural shift. People began to understand each other's roles better, leading to increased empathy, collaboration, and respect across departments. Within months, productivity jumped 15%, and employee morale soared. That team, once riddled with uncertainty, became one of the most stable and confident units I ever led.

In Miami and West Palm Beach, we collaborated with local schools and businesses to host a series of community events, career talks, and leadership workshops. These initiatives went far beyond traditional branding. They gave our employees a reason to be proud. They got to share their knowledge, mentor students, and represent the company as ambassadors in their communities. Customers began to take notice of our deeper involvement, which led to stronger loyalty and increased foot traffic. Internally, our team felt a renewed sense of purpose. One employee said, "For the first time, I feel like I'm part of something that matters." That pride translated into lower absenteeism, higher retention, and a more cohesive, values-driven team.

I also recall an initiative in Florida, where our Restaurant team served customers from local companies. Many workers from these local companies felt like just another face in the crowd—unseen and unappreciated. We introduced a simple recognition program where team members remembered and used customers' names, celebrated birthdays with small gestures, and created a "Wall of Gratitude" where customers could leave notes about employees who made their day better. The result? A surge in emotional connection and loyalty—not just from customers, but from staff as well. The sense of pride in service elevated everyone involved.

These experiences reaffirmed a powerful truth: when leaders intentionally create ways for people to give, grow, and feel seen, they unleash untapped levels of energy, purpose, and performance. Adding value is not always flashy—it's often in the consistent, human-centered gestures that make people feel significant.

Conclusion

The Key of Adding Value is about enriching every space you lead in—your people, your customers, and your organization. It requires intention, humility, and the willingness to pour into others with no immediate guarantee of return. But over time, it builds something far more powerful than performance metrics: it builds legacy.

This Key is what brings true fulfillment to my life. It's the joy of helping others grow. It took me many years to find people who genuinely wanted to add value to my life—and now I strive to be that person for others. I believe this is where real leaders live from: not power or position, but a deep commitment to elevating others.

At the end of the day, businesses may rise or fall, organizations may flourish or flounder, families may go through seasons—but the value we add to others will be the legacy that stays with us when we leave this planet. And the truth is, when we truly live from this Key, the chances of our families, businesses, teams, and even our communities flourishing increase exponentially. Adding value is not just a principle—it's a way of life that creates lasting impact.

Key Takeaways

Great leaders add value in every interaction. Whether through development, recognition, coaching, or service, value-adding leaders create momentum, trust, and cultures that last. Below are the core insights from this Key, expanded for deeper reflection:

1. Adding value begins with seeing people. When leaders take the time to understand the unique strengths, struggles, and goals of their team members, they unlock deeper trust and loyalty.

2. Coaching transforms potential into performance. It's not just about correcting mistakes—it's about creating space for growth, learning, and self-discovery. Coaching empowers people to solve problems, make decisions, and build confidence.

3. Customer loyalty grows from consistency and care. Every interaction is an opportunity to exceed expectations and build emotional connection. People remember how they were made to feel long after the transaction is complete.

4. People-centered leadership drives lasting growth. Business outcomes are sustained when people feel valued, equipped, and empowered. Culture eats strategy for breakfast—and value-driven culture starts at the top.

5. Culture-building requires systems, tools, and intention. Recognition programs, development calendars, and feed-

back loops aren't just nice-to-haves—they're structural reinforcements for your values.

6. Legacy is built through consistent, humble investment in others. Your greatest influence is not in what you do for yourself, but in how you multiply growth in others. True legacy is living in such a way that others rise simply because they were near you.

7. Small actions create exponential impact. A kind word, a moment of listening, a handwritten note—these seemingly minor moments compound over time to create loyalty, transformation, and legacy.

8. Adding value is a mindset, not a strategy. It's not something you turn on when convenient. It's a lifestyle of leadership grounded in service, generosity, and purpose.

Reflective Questions

1. Where in your leadership can you increase your efforts to intentionally add value to others?

2. How often do you coach, recognize, or support your team in ways that feel personal and meaningful?

3. What systems or tools can you implement to make value-adding practices part of your team's culture?

4. How can you ensure that your leadership legacy is rooted in helping others grow?

5. What adjustments can you make to better balance your own growth while consistently investing in your people? Where

are the greatest opportunities for you to add value right now—in your team, your service, or your organization?

6. What daily habits can you implement to ensure you're regularly recognizing and appreciating those around you?

7. How can you equip others to add value themselves, creating a ripple effect of leadership and excellence?

Mirror: Looking Within – The Key of Adding Value

Take a moment to sit with this truth: You have the power to make others feel seen, valued, and empowered—every single day. That power doesn't require a title or a budget. It begins with your presence, your words, your willingness to listen, and your intentional actions.

Ask yourself:

- Do the people around me feel enriched because of my leadership?

- Am I building people or simply managing them?

- Do I walk into a room thinking, "How can I give?" or "What can I get?"

- Who needs encouragement, who has untapped potential, who's been quietly consistent and deserves recognition?

True value-adding leaders are tuned in to the humanity of others. They don't lead for applause—they lead to awaken greatness. Who will be better because you showed up today?

Chapter 11

The Key of 7x Advanced Leadership

"A good leader seeks the Lord, commits their way to Him, and leads with a servant's heart, reflecting His purpose." – Inspired by Proverbs 16:3

The Key of 7x Advanced Leadership represents the culmination of the previous nine keys—each one important on its own, but together capable of exponential impact when fueled by a deeper connection to purpose, belief, and spiritual grounding. This key is about multiplying your influence through intentional alignment with your highest calling, whether you describe that as faith in God, the law of attraction, or an unwavering belief in your mission.

The Foundation of Faith in Leadership

Throughout my leadership journey, faith in God has been my compass and source of strength. During the most uncertain moments—financial setbacks, team struggles, or personal crossroads—it was my spiritual grounding that brought clarity, peace, and renewed confidence. Leadership can be a lonely road, but knowing I am guided by something greater has helped me push forward with courage.

One defining moment came during a significant financial crisis while managing a company I was leading. Revenue was plummeting, operational costs rising, and external pressures mounting. Amid the chaos, I turned to prayer. That moment of stillness gave me clarity: I restructured key operations, renegotiated with vendors, and reignited the belief of my team. We didn't just survive—we came back stronger.

Faith as the Multiplier of the Nine Keys

Faith isn't a standalone idea—it acts as an amplifier for everything we've learned so far:

1. **The Key of the Mirror:** Faith helps you self-reflect with honesty and grace. It allows you to grow without guilt and to lead without ego.

2. **The Key of Direction:** Faith offers internal GPS. When goals align with purpose, clarity comes faster.

3. **The Key of Self-Belief:** Believing in God (or higher purpose) strengthens belief in yourself. You lead with conviction.

4. **The Key of Great Communication:** Faith fosters empathy. It softens your words while sharpening your message.

5. **The Key of Follow-Up:** Faith builds patience and persistence. It reminds you that progress is often invisible at first.

6. **The Key of Recruiting with the End in Mind:** Faith gives discernment. You see beyond résumés into character and long-term alignment.

7. **The Key of Trust:** Faith makes you trustworthy. When you live with integrity, your team feels safe to follow you.

8. **The Key of Living from Solutions:** Faith reframes problems. You see challenges as assignments, not setbacks.

9. **The Key of Adding Value:** Faith roots you in service. You lead not for position but for impact.

If faith, religion, or belief systems are not part of your personal journey, consider replacing the word "God" with "purpose," "universe," or "unshakable belief." The principle still stands: when your leadership is rooted in something bigger than your ego, your influence multiplies.

Overcoming Leadership Challenges with Faith

Faith gives you fuel when logic runs dry. During times of loss, layoffs, missed targets, or public criticism, it's easy to spiral into fear or self-doubt. But when you lead from faith, you remember who you are and why you started. It grounds your decisions in courage rather than fear.

In a staffing crisis at a regional company, the pressure to cut corners and compromise values was intense. But through prayer and reflection, I stayed centered and made tough calls with confidence. Those decisions not only protected the team but inspired long-term loyalty and growth.

There are also moments in leadership where the challenge ahead seems impossible—where no clear answer exists and hope feels distant. In these moments, the ability to lean on God provides a foundation that transcends circumstance. When you place your trust in Him, even when there seems to be no hope or solution, something powerful happens. Faith with action activates insight. Clarity appears. Doors open that you couldn't have imagined. What seemed like a dead end transforms into a new beginning.

I've experienced this time and time again—when resources were thin, when pressure mounted, and when fear tried to take over. But by remaining grounded in faith and stepping forward with courage, I've seen God illuminate solutions that were invisible just moments before. He brings opportunities disguised in setbacks and wisdom in the waiting.

Faith also guides your tone during difficult conversations. It reminds you to correct without condemnation, and to lead with love even when accountability is necessary. It helps you stay composed, humble, and solution-focused when others may react emotionally. And it reassures you that you're not leading alone—you are being led while leading others.

The Principle of 7x Multiplication

The idea of 7x leadership is simple but powerful: when you lead from spiritual grounding, your influence multiplies far beyond what effort alone could accomplish. This is not linear growth—this is exponential multiplication. It affects not only what you do, but how you do it and who you inspire along the way.

1. Your words carry more weight because they're rooted in wisdom, not ego.

2. Your presence calms storms because you're grounded in peace, not panic.

3. Your decisions create ripple effects because they align with something greater than profits—they're driven by purpose.

4. Your legacy becomes generational because people don't just remember your success—they remember how you made them feel, grow, and believe.

While leading a district in Florida, I implemented not just business strategy but purpose-driven leadership. We partnered with community organizations, invested in team development, and connected our goals with service. Revenue grew, turnover dropped, and the workplace culture became magnetic. That's the power of 7x leadership—purpose in action. What starts in the boardroom flows into families, communities, and future generations.

When you lead with faith, you're not just building a business—you're building people, and people build everything else.

Practical Ways to Lead with Faith

1. **Start with Quiet Time:** Begin each day with reflection, prayer, or meditation. Clarity often comes in the quiet.

2. **Pray Before Big Decisions:** Ask for wisdom and listen. Even a few minutes can bring powerful direction.

3. **Speak Life:** Use your words to uplift. Speak blessings over your team, your goals, and your challenges.

4. **Lead as a Servant:** Put your people first. Practice humility, compassion, and generosity.

5. **Surround Yourself with Faith-Builders:** Connect with mentors or peers who reinforce your values.

6. **Acknowledge God (or Higher Power) Publicly:** Let your team see where your strength comes from. It inspires more than you know.

Faith and Resilience

Faith makes you resilient because it shifts your focus. Instead of asking, "Why me?" you start asking, "What's the lesson here? What's the assignment?" You become a leader who doesn't just react—you rise.

During the COVID-19 pandemic, many leaders panicked. I chose prayer. We pivoted business models, kept people employed, and even innovated new offerings. That season tested every leadership principle in this book. And faith carried me through every one of them.

Conclusion

The Key of 7x Advanced Leadership is about leading with power, peace, and purpose. Faith in God, or deep spiritual belief, doesn't eliminate adversity. It equips you to lead through it with grace. It transforms you from a person who influences to a leader who multiplies impact.

You don't need to be perfect to lead powerfully. You need to be *anchored*. And faith is that anchor.

In my life, this Key has transformed everything. It has elevated my mindset, my relationships, my results, and my leadership. I share it openly with my teams, because I know its power firsthand. You may call it God, belief, energy, or vision—but when you tap into it, you don't just lead... you elevate everyone around you.

Key Takeaways

Faith multiplies leadership. When your foundation is strong, your influence becomes limitless. When you lead with belief, purpose, and service, the 9 Keys are no longer just strategies—they become a way of life.

1. **Faith turns obstacles into opportunities.** It allows you to navigate storms with perspective and peace.

2. **Spiritual grounding expands your leadership vision.** You stop seeing through fear and begin operating from clarity.

3. **Purpose-driven leadership attracts commitment.** Teams rally behind a leader who leads from conviction, not control.

4. **7x leadership is contagious.** When your leadership is multiplied by faith, your people grow in courage, resilience, and ownership.

5. **Legacy grows where faith leads.** When you anchor your leadership in belief and service, the results transcend what you can measure.

Reflective Questions

1. In what areas of your leadership do you need to lean more on faith than on control?

2. How can you use your spiritual beliefs to guide your actions and lift your team during difficult seasons?

3. What would change in your leadership if you started every challenge by asking, "What's the assignment here?"

4. How can you model purpose-driven leadership that inspires exponential impact beyond results?

5. Who in your life could benefit from seeing faith in action through your leadership? How can you root your leadership more deeply in your personal faith, values, or purpose?

6. What spiritual or belief-based practices can you incorporate into your leadership rhythm?

7. In what ways can you encourage your team by modeling resilience, clarity, and purpose-driven leadership?

8. How can you elevate your leadership beyond results and into lasting impact?

Mirror: Looking Within – The Key of 7x Advanced Leadership

Pause. Breathe. Let the noise fall away for a moment.

Leadership isn't always loud. Sometimes, the greatest strength is found in stillness. This final Key invites you to stop striving long enough to ask:

Am I leading with force... or with faith?

You've unlocked powerful tools—mirror, direction, self-belief, end in mind, communication, trust, follow-up, living from solutions, value. But this Key reminds you that your leadership becomes limitless when it's aligned with something greater than yourself. Faith—whether in God, purpose, or divine order—doesn't just strengthen your steps... it multiplies them.

Look in the mirror and ask:

1. Do I believe I have to figure it all out alone—or do I trust I'm being guided?

2. When challenges come, do I anchor myself in prayer, reflection, or purpose—or do I react from fear?

3. Am I relying on logic and control, or am I creating space for divine insight and inspired action?

Leadership rooted in ego can achieve success. Leadership rooted in faith creates legacy.

This is the shift: from hustle to harmony. From pressure to peace. From surviving to multiplying.

Now ask yourself:

1. What might open up in my leadership if I led with belief, not just boldness?

2. What would change if I began each challenge by asking, "What's the assignment here?"

3. Who around me needs to see faith in action—and how can I be that example?

You don't need to be perfect. You need to be anchored.

When you lead from deep conviction and spiritual alignment, your presence becomes a force of calm, clarity, and courage. You stop just influencing outcomes—you begin transforming lives.

And that's what 7x leadership is all about.

Chapter 12

Final Reflection: The Heart Behind This Book

I want to take a moment to acknowledge that this book would not be possible without the influence of the many people who have walked beside me throughout my life and leadership journey. My family, my friends, my mentors, and the incredible individuals I've had the privilege of working with—each of you have helped shape the leader I continue to become.

This book is a reflection of those shared experiences—and more importantly, it's written for you. The reader who is searching, striving, and maybe even struggling to become a stronger leader. My hope is that these pages help you realize what I've come to learn through decades of leadership: anyone can grow into a leader.

Yes, some people may seem to be born with natural leadership traits. But leadership, at its core, is not a birthright—it is a decision. It is a skill. It's learned, developed, and refined through reflection, courage, and the willingness to keep growing.

Some of you may be thinking, "But I'm not leading anyone." Let me challenge that thought. You may not hold a formal title—but if you're a parent, a sibling, a friend, a coach, a teammate, or a role model in any way, you are already leading.

The most difficult person I've ever had to lead was myself. And learning to lead yourself with discipline, vision, and integrity is the true foundation of leading others.

Leadership is not about titles. Titles may give someone a position—but real leadership is earned through influence. As my mentor John C. Maxwell says, and as I've found to be absolutely true:

"Leadership is influence. Nothing more, nothing less."

So whether you're leading a team of hundreds—or just learning to lead yourself—this book is my gift to you. It's a roadmap. A mirror. A motivator.

Thank you for taking this journey with me.

Now go lead—with purpose, with courage, and with the unwavering belief that your influence can change the world.

Chapter 13

About the Author

James Rodriguez is a transformational leader, U.S. Coast Guard veteran, award-winning executive, and leadership coach with decades of experience turning around businesses, building winning teams, and helping others unlock their leadership potential.

From growing up in East Harlem to launching high-performing teams across the United States and Latin America, James's journey is one of grit, growth, and grace. His leadership philosophy is built not on theory, but on real-life experience—earned on the streets, in the military, and in the boardroom.

Throughout his career, James has held leadership positions in the retail, restaurant, and hospitality industries, rising from frontline manager to President and CEO. His hands-on approach, deep understanding of team dynamics, and commitment to adding value have made him a sought-after consultant and speaker across international markets.

James integrates timeless leadership principles with his personal faith and life lessons to empower others. His passion is helping people grow—personally, professionally, and spiritually.

Today, James continues to lead, coach, and serve with one mission in mind: to help others discover the leader within and multiply their influence through purpose-driven leadership.

Chapter 14

Thank You

We want to sincerely thank you for taking the time to read this book and allowing us the opportunity to add value to you and your team.

We would also love to hear how this book has impacted your leadership journey or added value to your life. **Your story matters to us.**

If you're interested in having James speak at your event or lead a customized leadership training for your organization, we would love to connect.

Please reach out to us at: info@leadershipunlockedthebook.com

We believe great leadership transforms lives, teams, and companies—and we'd be honored to partner with you on that journey.

Made in the USA
Columbia, SC
10 June 2025